UNDERSTANDING AND USING ADVANCED STATISTICS

UNDERSTANDING AND USING ADVANCED STATISTICS

Jeremy Foster
Emma Barkus
Christian Yavorsky

SAGE Publications
London ● Thousand Oaks ● New Delhi

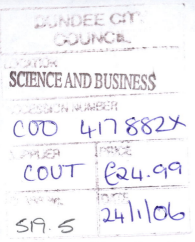
 SAGE Publications Ltd
1 Oliver's Yard
55 City Road
London EC1Y 1SP

SAGE Publications Inc.
2455 Teller Road
Thousand Oaks, California 91320

SAGE Publications India Pvt Ltd
B-42, Panchsheel Enclave
Post Box 4109
New Delhi 110 017

British Library Cataloguing in Publication data

A catalogue record for this book is available from the
British Library

ISBN 1 4129 0013 1
ISBN 1 4129 0014 X (pbk)

Library of Congress Control Number: 2005929180

Typeset by C&M Digitals (P) Ltd, Chennai, India
Printed on paper from sustainable resources
Printed in Great Britain by The Cromwell Press Ltd, Trowbridge, Wiltshire

Summary of Contents

Contents

Basic Features of Statistical Analysis and the General Linear Model

INTRODUCTION

The aim of this book is to describe some of the statistical techniques which are becoming increasingly common, particularly in the social sciences. The spread of sophisticated computer packages and the machinery on which to run them has meant that procedures which were previously only available to experienced researchers with access to expensive machines and research students can now be carried out in a few seconds by almost every undergraduate. The tendency of the packages to produce items of output which are unfamiliar to most users has lead to modifications in the content of quantitative data analysis courses, but this has not always meant that students gain an understanding of what the analytic procedures do, when they should be used and what the results provided signify. Our aim has been to provide the basis for gaining such an understanding. There are many texts and Internet resources covering the material which we do, but our experience is that many of them are too advanced, starting at too high a level and including topics such as matrix algebra which leave many students baffled. What we have attempted to provide is an assistant which will help you make the transition from the simpler statistics (*t*-tests, analysis of variance) to more complex procedures; we are hoping we have translated the more technical texts into a form which matches your understanding. Each chapter provides an outline of the statistical technique, the type of question it answers, what the results produced tell you and gives examples from published literature of how the technique has been used.

In recent years there has been a considerable growth in the use of qualitative research methods in many areas of social science including psychology and nursing and this has been accompanied by a decline in the previous preponderance of quantitative research. One feature of the qualitative research movement has been an emphasis upon the ethical issues involved in carrying out research involving people, the need to recognise that the participants own their data and that they should have an input – even perhaps a veto – over the interpretations made of it and the uses to which it is put. This concern has rejuvenated the ethical debate within quantitative research and brought back an awareness of the need to ensure that participants give informed consent to taking part, that they are not studied unknowingly or covertly, that they have the right to confidentiality and anonymity. This is not the place to discuss the ethics of research, but it is only proper that we should urge those considering quantitative research to be aware of the ethical guidelines applicable to their discipline and ensure they abide by them. Gathering the data which lends itself to quantitative analysis is not a value-free activity even if 'number crunching' may in itself appear to be so.

Before describing the more complex statistical techniques, we begin by recapitulating the basics of statistical analysis, reminding you of the analysis of variance and outlining the principles of the general linear model (GLM) which underpins many of the techniques described later.

BASIC FEATURES OF STATISTICAL ANALYSIS

Experiments or correlational research designs

In an experiment using a between-subjects design, the participants are randomly allocated to different levels of the independent variable and if all other variables are controlled by being kept constant or by the design of the experiment then it is assumed that any differences in the dependent variable measures are due to the independent variable. (This is a gross simplification of how to design an experiment!) But in many or even most fields of investigation it is impossible to carry out a true experiment because it is impossible to control the conditions, impossible to allocate participants randomly to conditions or ethically unacceptable to do so. One is then forced to consider an alternative type of investigation such as a pseudo-experiment or a correlational study in which data on independent and dependent variables is collected (often simultaneously) and the relationships between them are investigated.

Experiments typically involve analysing the data for differences: did group A score differently from group B on the dependent variable? Correlational studies usually involve analysing the data for correlations or associations: did those who scored highly on measure X also obtain high scores on measure Y?

Independent and dependent variables

Independent variables are those aspects of the respondents or cases which you anticipate will affect the output measure, the dependent variable. An independent variable is often the 'grouping' variable which divides people, respondents or cases into separate groups. This division may be based on experimental conditions or it may be some characteristic of the participants such as their age group, sex, economic status. When the independent variable involves different participants in each group, it is referred to as a between-subjects variable. Alternatively, the independent variable may be a number of experimental conditions where all participants take part in every condition. If this is the case, the variable is a within-subjects factor and a repeated measures design is being used. A mixed design is where there are at least two independent variables, and one is between subjects while one is within subjects.

The dependent variable is usually a continuous variable such as a measure of performance on an experimental task or a score on a questionnaire which the researcher proposes is affected by the independent variables. In some types of research, the dependent variable is categorical, which means participants are divided into categories such as surviving and not surviving or relapsing and not relapsing. The data is then frequencies: how many people fall into each category? The research may be concerned with finding which factors predict category membership, and then logistic regression may be used to analyse the data.

It is important not to confuse variables with their levels. An independent variable is the experimental manipulation or the dimension upon which the participants are categorised. For example, suppose we were testing the ability of boys and girls to do mental arithmetic when they were distracted by background noise which could be loud, quiet or not present at all. We would design the experiment so that our participants carried out a mental arithmetic task with loud noise, with quiet noise or without noise. There would be two independent variables: participant sex (male or female) and noise condition (loud, quiet, absent). The first independent variable has two levels (male or female) and the second independent variable has three levels. So this would be a 2×3 (or 3×2 since it does not matter in which order the numbers here are presented) experiment. The expression 2×3 contains two digits, showing there are two independent variables. The actual digits, 2 and 3, indicate that one of the variables has two levels and the other has three levels.

Types of data

There are essentially two types of data, frequency and numerical, depending on the type of measurement scale used. One type of measurement scale is categorical or nominal, where cases are allocated to categories such as 'male' and 'female', or 'recovering after 2 months', 'recovering after 6 months', 'not recovering'. This yields frequency data which is obtained if you count the number of cases or people in each category. The other type of measurement scale is quantitative or numerical: here you are measuring not how many people or cases fall into a particular category, but how much or how well they performed by assigning a numerical value to their performance, for example by recording the time taken to do a task or the number of questions answered.

In a nominal scale, the number is simply functioning as a label and the size of the number does not reflect the magnitude or order of the items. Telephone numbers are an example of a nominal scale, since the size of the number does not reflect anything about the size or order of the people who have those numbers. Similarly, in the example of performance under conditions of background noise described earlier, you might designate the loud noise condition as condition 1, the quiet noise condition as condition 2 and the no-noise condition as condition 3. Here the numbers are acting just as convenient labels for each condition or category and their size means nothing. When you have counted the number of cases in each category, you have frequency data which can be analysed using procedures such as chi-square, log–linear analysis or logistic regression.

Numerical data can be measured on a ratio, interval or ordinal scale. In a ratio scale there is a true zero and a number which is twice as large as another reflects the fact that the attribute being measured is twice as great. Ratio scales are rare in the social sciences unless one is using a measure of some physical feature such as height or time: someone who is 2 metres tall is twice as tall as someone who is 1 metre tall; someone who took 30 seconds to do a task took twice as long as someone who did it in 15 seconds. In an interval scale, the difference between two values at one point on the scale is the same as the difference between two equidistant values at another point on the scale: the usual example cited is the Fahrenheit scale where the difference between 15 and 20 degrees is the same as the difference between 5 and 10 degrees. There are few cases of interval scales in the social sciences (e.g. IQ is not an interval scale because the difference between an IQ of 100 and 105 is not the same as the difference between 70 and 75), although many examples of data being treated as though it were an interval scale. In an ordinal or rank scale, the size of the numbers reflects the order of the items as in a race where first came before second and second before third. But this information tells you nothing about the intervals between the scale points: first may have been just in front of second with third trailing far behind. In practice, the distinction between ratio and interval scales is widely ignored but ordinal or rank data is treated differently by using non-parametric procedures.

Non-parametric and parametric analyses

There are two groups of statistical techniques: parametric and non-parametric. Non-parametric techniques are considered distribution free, meaning that they do not involve any assumptions about the distribution of the population from which the sample of dependent variable measures is drawn. (It does not, for example, have to be normally distributed.) Non-parametric techniques are used with frequency data and when the dependent variable has been measured on an ordinal (rank) scale. If the dependent variable has been measured on an interval scale but does not fulfil certain assumptions described below, it can be transformed into ordinal data and the non-parametric techniques can then be applied.

The parametric tests are generally considered more powerful, offer greater flexibility in analysis and address a greater number of research questions. The majority of the statistical techniques outlined in this book require that the dependent variable measures meet the requirements for being parametric data, which are:

1 the dependent variable is measured on either an interval or a ratio scale;
2 scores on the dependent variable approximate to a normal distribution or are drawn from a population where the variable can be assumed to be normally distributed;
3 scores on the dependent variable show homogeneity of variance between groups of participants.

Regarding point 1, strictly speaking parametric analysis should only be performed on continuous interval or ratio data but in practice many types of data are taken to be interval even if one could reasonably argue that they are not. An example is where a Likert scale has been used to measure attitudes. This is where participants are presented with a statement such as 'The death penalty is morally acceptable' and indicate their response by indicating how far they agree or disagree with it using a five- or seven-point scale with one end of the scale indicating 'strongly agree', and the other indicating 'strongly disagree'. If the data is ordinal (ranks), then non-parametric analysis is needed.

Concerning point 2, parametric statistical analysis is based on the assumption that the scores come from a normal distribution, meaning that if one could obtain the scores from the population then they would be normally distributed. Of course one does not know the distribution in the population, only the distribution in the sample one has. So it is necessary to check whether these approximate to a normal distribution. This can be done by plotting the distribution and examining it to see if it is more or less normal. The shape of the distribution can be evaluated in terms of skewness and kurtosis. Skewness reflects the positioning of the peak of the curve (is it in the centre?) and kurtosis refers to the height of the tails of the curve (is the curve too flat?). Statistical packages may give indices of skew and kurtosis; the values should be close to zero.

On point 3, homogeneity of variance is the assumption that the amount of variance is the same in the different sets of scores of the participants. It can be assessed using Levene's test for homogeneity of variance which gives a t value: if t is significant, the groups differ in their variances, that is there is heterogeneity of variance. If you are comparing groups of equal size, heterogeneity of variance is not important, but for groups of unequal sizes it needs to be dealt with. This can be done in a number of ways including transforming the scores, using a more stringent significance level (perhaps 0.01 rather than 0.05), applying a non-parametric procedure.

Statistical significance

Probability testing is at the centre of statistical analysis and is essentially concerned with deciding how probable it is that the results observed could have been due to chance or error variation in the scores. To make the explanation simpler, we shall take the case of testing to see whether there is a difference between two groups of respondents. Suppose we have measured the amount of concern people have with their body image using a questionnaire in which a high score indicates a high level of concern, and done this for a group of women and for a group of men. The null hypothesis states that there is no difference between the scores of the two groups. The research (or alternative) hypothesis states that there is a difference between the scores of the two groups. The research hypothesis may predict the direction of the outcome (e.g. women will have a higher score than the men) in which case it is a directional or one-tailed hypothesis. Or the research hypothesis may just predict a difference between the two groups, without specifying which direction that difference will take (e.g. women and men will score differently from one another) in which case it is referred to as a non-directional or two-tailed hypothesis.

In our example, we want to know how likely it is that the difference in the mean scores of the women and men was the result of chance variation in the scores. You will probably recognise this as a situation in which you would turn to the t-test, and may remember that in the t-test you calculate the difference between the means of the two groups and express it as a ratio of the standard error of the difference which is calculated from the variance in the scores. If this ratio is greater than a certain amount, which you can find from the table for t, you can conclude that the difference between the means is unlikely to have arisen from the chance variability in the data and that there is a 'significant' difference between the means.

It is conventional to accept that 'unlikely' means having a 5% (0.05) probability or less. So if the probability of the difference arising by chance is 0.05 or less, you conclude it did not arise by chance. There are occasions when one uses a more stringent probability or significance level and only accepts the difference as significant if the probability of its arising by chance is 1% (0.01) or less. Much more rarely, one may accept a less stringent probability level such as 10% (0.1).

In considering the level of significance which you are going to use, there are two types of errors which need to be borne in mind. A Type I error occurs when a researcher accepts the research hypothesis and incorrectly rejects the null hypothesis. A Type II error occurs when the null hypothesis is accepted and the research hypothesis is incorrectly rejected. When you use the 5% (0.05) significance level, you have a 5% chance of making a Type I error. You can reduce this by using a more stringent level such as 1% (0.01), but this increases the probability of making a Type II error.

When a number of significance tests are applied to a set of data it is generally considered necessary to apply some method of correcting for multiple testing. (If you carried out 100 *t*-tests, 5% of them are expected to come out 'significant' just by chance. So multiple significance testing can lead to accepting outcomes as significant when they are not, a Type I error.) To prevent the occurrence of a Type I error some researchers simply set the significance level needed to be reached at the 1% level, but this does seem rather arbitrary. A more precise correction for multiple testing is the Bonferroni correction in which the 0.05 probability level is divided by the number of times the same test is being used on the data set. For example, if four *t*-tests are being calculated on the same data set then 0.05 would be divided by 4 which would give a probability level of 0.0125 which would have to be met to achieve statistical significance.

RECAPITULATION OF ANALYSIS OF VARIANCE (ANOVA)

ANOVAs, like *t*-tests, examine the differences between group means. However, an ANOVA has greater flexibility than a *t*-test since the researcher is able to use more than two groups in the analysis. Additionally ANOVAs are able to consider the effect of more than one independent variable and to reveal whether the effect of one of them is influenced by the other: whether they interact.

Variance summarises the degree to which each score differs from the mean, and as implied by the name ANOVAs consider the amount of variance in a data set. Variance potentially arises from three sources: individual differences, error and the effect of the independent variable. The sources of variance in a set of data are expressed in the sum of squares value in an ANOVA. In a between-groups analysis of variance, the between-groups sum of squares represents the amount of variance accounted for by the effect of the independent variable with the estimate of error removed. The sums of squares are divided by the corresponding degrees of freedom to produce the mean square between groups and the mean square within groups. The ratio between these two figures produces a value for F. The further away from one the F value is, the lower the probability that the differences between the groups arose by chance and the higher the level of significance of the effect of the independent variable.

Repeated measures ANOVAs occur when the participants complete the same set of tasks under different conditions or in longitudinal studies where the same tasks are completed by the same participants on more than one occasion. There are additional requirements which need to be met in order to ensure that the

Table 1.1 Hypothetical data from an experiment comparing the effects of distracting noise on mental arithmetic performance for males and females

	Sex of participants	
Noise	*Males*	*Females*
Loud	9.46	10.34
Quiet	12.32	12.11
None	12.82	17.23

results from a repeated measures ANOVA are reliable. One of these is known as sphericity and tests for it are given in the output from the computerised statistical packages used to analyse data. If the test is significant, sphericity is a problem within the data. Sphericity is concerned with the similarity of the relationship between the dependent and independent variables in a repeated measures design. If the relationship between them changes over repeated measures of the dependent variable, the assumption of sphericity is violated and this will increase the chances of a Type I error occurring. To overcome violation of this assumption a stricter significance value can be set, or one can use corrections such as the Greenhouse–Geisser, Huynh–Feldt and lower bound epsilon formulae which adjust the degrees of freedom. (Statistical packages will print these adjusted degrees of freedom.)

Main effects, simple effects, interaction

Our hypothetical experiment on boys and girls doing mental arithmetic with loud background noise, quiet noise or no noise would yield six means as illustrated in Table 1.1, where the numbers represent the number of mental arithmetic problems solved and have just been made up for the purpose of helping us explain some of the concepts. One would anticipate using analysis of variance to analyse a set of data like this.

When using ANOVA models, terms such as main effects, interactions and simple effects are encountered. It is worth reminding ourselves what these mean (especially as the concept of interactions seems to baffle many students).

A significant main effect demonstrates that an independent variable influences the dependent variable. In this example, a significant main effect of noise would establish that there was a difference between the overall means for the three noise conditions of loud, quiet and none. However, it does not establish which of the independent variable groups are significantly different from one another. Is the loud condition significantly different from the quiet condition? Is it significantly different from the none condition? Is the quiet condition significantly different

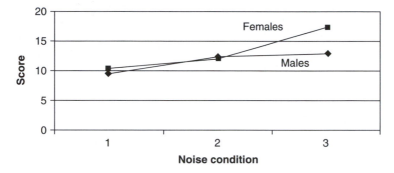

Figure 1.1   Graph of the (hypothetical) data from Table 1.1 showing an interaction

from the none condition? These questions are answered by testing the differences between the particular pairs of means of the groups using a priori or *post hoc* tests.

Whether to use a priori or *post hoc* tests depends on whether the researcher has previously stated the hypotheses to test. If you have honestly stated beforehand the comparisons between individual pairs of means which you intend to make, then you are entitled to use an a priori test such as a *t*-test. If you have looked at the data and then decided it looks worth comparing one mean with another, you have to use a *post hoc* test such as Newman–Keuls, Tukey or Scheffé.

An interaction occurs when the effect of one independent variable is affected by another independent variable. In our example, the difference between males and females seems to be greater in the none noise condition than it is in the loud or quiet conditions. This would be an interaction: the magnitude of the differences between levels on one variable (sex) is influenced by the level on the other variable (noise). (An interaction can be shown graphically if you plot the data as shown in Figure 1.1. The lines representing the data for the two sexes are not parallel, and this suggests an interaction.) Interactions can be two way, three way or more complex depending on the number of independent variables combining to have an effect on the dependent variable. A two-way interaction will contain two independent variables (as in our example), a three-way interaction will contain three, etc.

A simple effect refers to the effect of one independent variable at one particular level of the other independent variable. For example, in the data shown in Table 1.1, it looks as though there is a difference between the sexes under the none noise condition but not under the loud or quiet conditions. You could test the differences between the sexes for each noise condition separately, and would then be testing simple effects. Usually you only look at simple effects if you have found a significant interaction.

An example of ANOVA, which is frequently used in research, is provided by Burgess et al. (2003) who measured attachment style between young children

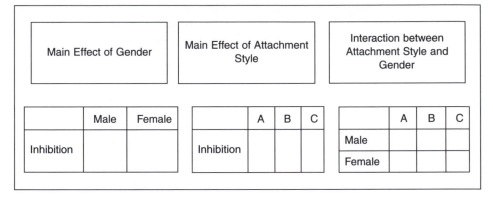

Figure 1.2 The ANOVA considering the effect of attachment style and gender on oral inhibition in a group of children considered in Burgess et al. (2003)

and their parents at 14 months of age and classified the children into three attachment style groups: insecure–avoidant (A), securely attached (B) and insecure–ambivalent (C). ANOVA was used to examine the effects of attachment style on oral inhibition measured at 24 months. Burgess et al. also entered gender into the model as they thought that it may be an additional factor which could influence oral inhibition. (Including gender in the analysis demonstrates a useful aspect of ANOVA: it allows a consideration of extraneous variables, namely uncontrollable variables which may influence the outcome measure.) So this was a 2 × 3 between-groups ANOVA. The aspects of the data considered by this ANOVA are demonstrated in Figure 1.2.

The authors reported that gender did not have a significant main effect on oral inhibition nor did it interact with attachment style, so the analysis was repeated with gender removed. They reported a trend for a main effect of attachment group on oral inhibition. Since the hypothesis which they made regarding the effect of attachment style on oral inhibition was one tailed (i.e. they had pre-dicted the direction of the relationship), they performed *post hoc* analysis to determine whether the directional nature of the relationship was found even though the main effect was only significant at a trend level. When considering their *post hoc* analysis, the authors reported the mean difference between the groups which proved to be significantly different from one another.

THE GENERAL LINEAR MODEL

The general linear model (GLM) is not a discrete statistical technique itself but the statistical theory which underpins many parametric techniques. The general aim of methods underpinned by the GLM is to determine whether the independent variable(s) affect or relate to the dependent variable(s). The GLM is summarized by the regression equation which is:

$$Y = c + bX$$

In the equation c is the value of Y when X is zero, and b is the slope of the curve or the amount by which X must be multiplied to give the value of Y.

The equation basically means that the dependent variable, Y, is related to the independent variable X. The fundamental notion that the dependent variable is related to the independent variable also applies to the ANOVA. When you are comparing the means of groups of respondents, as in the example of arithmetic performance under different levels of background noise mentioned earlier, you are actually proposing that the levels of the independent variable affect the dependent variable. So analysis of variance can be seen as a form of regression, and regression, correlation and the comparison of means in the ANOVA share the same underlying concepts. This is why we can say we have a general model. Whichever GLM technique is being used, it is assumed that the relationship between the independent and dependent variables is linear in nature – and so we have the notion of a GLM.

When variables are entered into one of the statistical techniques which use the GLM, it is assumed they have an additive effect, which means they each contribute to the prediction of the dependent variable. For example, when three variables are placed into a regression model (or equation) the second variable adds to the predictive value of the first, and the third adds to the predictive value of the second and first combined. (The independent contribution of each variable is assessed by considering the additional variance accounted for or explained by the model when each variable is added.)

When do you need the GLM?

The GLM underlies a number of commonly used statistical techniques. Those which are explained in this book are:

Analysis of variance (ANOVA)
Analysis of covariance (ANCOVA)
Multivariate analysis of variance (MANOVA)
Multivariate analysis of covariance (MANCOVA)
Regression
Multiple regression
Log–linear analysis
Logistic regression

Factor analysis
Structural equation modelling
Survival analysis

ANOVA examines differences between three or more groups of participants or conditions. There is at least one independent variable, which consists of different categories, and a numerical (continuous) dependent variable. (In the example used earlier, mental arithmetic scores formed the dependent variable. Sex of participant and level of background noise formed the independent variables.) The ANOVA determines whether the amount of variance between the groups is greater than the variance within the groups; that is, whether the effect of the independent variable is greater than the effect of individual differences. In an independent measures (between-subjects) design, different participants take part in each condition. ANOVA can be used in repeated measures (within-subjects) studies where the same subjects take part in all of the experimental conditions and when a study has used a mixed design, where some of the independent variables are within subjects and some are between subjects.

ANCOVA is an extension of ANOVA in which a covariate, another relevant variable for which data is available, is classed as an additional independent variable. ANCOVA allows the researcher to 'control' for the effect of the additional variable(s) which may have had an impact on the outcome. For example, Bautmans et al. (2004) used an ANCOVA to examine whether the age of the participants was a potential covariate for the relationship they had found between the health category of elderly respondents and distance walked in 6 minutes. Even after correcting for age using the ANCOVA, the distance walked in 6 minutes decreased with health category so the authors concluded that the existence of pathology rather than increasing age was responsible for decreasing the exercise capacity of the elderly.

MANOVA and MANCOVA are extensions of ANOVA and ANCOVA which are used when there are multiple continuous dependent variables in the analysis.

Regression involves correlations, which are concerned with the relationship between pairs of variables. The type of data determines the correlation which it is appropriate to use. Pearson's product moment coefficient is a parametric correlation which expresses the relationship between two numerical continuous variables. If there is at least one dichotomous variable, the point biserial is appropriate. One would use this, for example, to correlate height with sex. When both variables are dichotomous, such as correlating sex with whether people are or are not smokers, the phi-correlation is required.

In multiple regression there is a single dependent variable predicted from a number of independent variables. Two-group logistic regression is an extension of multiple regression which is used when the dependent variable is dichotomous. Polychotomous logistic regression is necessary if the dependent variable consists of more than two categories.

Log–linear analysis is used to analyse contingency tables or cross-tabulations where more than two variables are included. (If there are just two variables, the chi-square test is often appropriate.)

Logistic regression analysis predicts the values of one dependent variable from one or more independent (predicting) variables when the dependent variable is dichotomous (meaning that it divides the respondents or cases into two exclusive groups such as having a particular illness or not having it). It is used to identify which predictor variables do predict the outcome.

Factor analysis and principal components analysis are a group of techniques which seek to reduce a large number of variables (e.g. questionnaire items or the diagnostic criteria for a psychiatric illness) to a few factors or components.

Structural equation modelling includes a number of statistical techniques and is referred to by a variety of names: causal modelling, causal analysis, simultaneous equation modelling, analysis of covariance structures. It is the most flexible statistical approach using the GLM and is able to deal with multiple independent and dependent variables of categorical or continuous data. Two analytic techniques which use structural equation modelling, path analysis and confirmatory factor analysis, are considered discrete types of this analysis.

Survival analysis is also known (rather perversely) as failure analysis. In medicine, it may be used to examine how long it takes before cancer patients go into remission when receiving one type of treatment versus another. In industry it is used to examine the length of time taken for a component to fail under particular conditions. It can take into account many independent variables such as demographics, environmental conditions, treatment received, etc., depending on the research question.

SUMMARY

In an experiment, participants are randomly allocated to different conditions which form the different levels of the independent variable. In a correlational study, participants are not randomly allocated to different conditions; data on the independent and dependent variables is collected for the respondents and the relationships between them are investigated.

There are two types of data: frequency and numerical. Frequency data involves counting how many people fall into a particular category. Numerical data involves measuring how well people performed by assigning a numerical value to their performance.

ANOVAs examine the differences between group means when there are more than two groups, are able to consider the effect of more than one independent variable and can reveal whether the effect of one of them is influenced by the other.

The general linear model (GLM) is a statistical theory which underpins many parametric analytic techniques. The general aim of methods underpinned by the GLM is to determine whether the independent variable(s) affect or relate to the dependent variable(s).

GLOSSARY

Dependent variable   the output measure of performance.

Frequency data   a count of the number of cases or people in each category.

Homogeneity of variance   when the amount of variance is the same in the different sets of scores of the participants.

Independent variable   those aspects of the respondents, which may be the experimental condition they undergo, which are anticipated will affect the dependent variable (output measure).

Interaction   when the effect of one independent variable is influenced by another independent variable.

Levels of an independent variable   the number of categories into which an independent variable has been divided.

Numerical data   obtained by measuring how well people performed by assigning a numerical value to their performance.

REFERENCES

Bautmans, I., Lambert, M. and Mets, T. (2004). The six-minute walk test in community dwelling elderly: influence of health status. *BMC Geriatrics*, 23, 6.
Burgess, K.B., Marshall, P.J., Rubin, K.H. and Fox, N.A. (2003). Infant attachment and temperament as predictors of subsequent externalizing problems and cardiac physiology. *Journal of Child Psychology and Psychiatry*, 44, 819–831.

FURTHER READING

Harris, R.J. (2001). *A Primer of Multivariate Statistics*. London: Lawrence Erlbaum.
Horton, R.L. (1978). *The General Linear Model: Data Analysis in the Social and Behavioral Sciences*. New York: McGraw-Hill.
Jamieson, J. (2004). Analysis of covariance (ANCOVA) with difference scores. *International Journal of Psychophysiology*, 52, 277–282.

Thompson, B. (1984). *Canonical Correlation Analysis: Uses and Interpretation*. Beverly Hills, CA: Sage.
Timm, N.H. (2002). *Applied Multivariate Analysis*. New York: Springer.

INTERNET SOURCES

http://www.statsoftinc.com/textbook/stglm.html
http://ibgwww.colorado.edu/~carey/p7291dir/handouts/glmtheory.pdf
http://name.math.univ-rennes1.fr/bernard.delyon/textbook/stglm.html

2

Multivariate Analysis of Variance

WHAT MULTIVARIATE ANALYSIS OF VARIANCE IS

The general purpose of multivariate analysis of variance (MANOVA) is to determine whether multiple levels of independent variables on their own or in combination with one another have an effect on the dependent variables. MANOVA requires that the dependent variables meet parametric requirements.

WHEN DO YOU NEED MANOVA?

MANOVA is used under the same circumstances as ANOVA but when there are multiple dependent variables as well as independent variables within the model which the researcher wishes to test. MANOVA is also considered a valid alternative to the repeated measures ANOVA when sphericity is violated.

WHAT KINDS OF DATA ARE NECESSARY?

The dependent variables in MANOVA need to conform to the parametric assumptions. Generally, it is better not to place highly correlated dependent variables in the same model for two main reasons. First, it does not make scientific sense to place into a model two or three dependent variables which the researcher knows measure the same aspect of outcome. (However, this point will be influenced by the hypothesis which the researcher is testing. For example, subscales from the same questionnaire may all be included in a MANOVA to overcome problems associated with multiple testing. Subscales from most questionnaires are related but may represent different aspects of the dependent variable.) The second reason for trying to avoid including highly correlated dependent variables is that the correlation between them can reduce the power of the tests. If

MANOVA is being used to reduce multiple testing, this loss in power needs to be considered as a trade-off for the reduction in the chance of a Type I error occurring.

Homogeneity of variance from ANOVA and *t*-tests becomes homogeneity of variance–covariance in MANOVA models. The amount of variance within each group needs to be comparable so that it can be assumed that the groups have been drawn from a similar population. Furthermore it is assumed that these results can be pooled to produce an error value which is representative of all the groups in the analysis. If there is a large difference in the amount of error within each group the estimated error measure for the model will be misleading.

HOW MUCH DATA?

There needs to be more participants than dependent variables. If there were only one participant in any one of the combination of conditions, it would be impossible to determine the amount of variance within that combination (since only one data point would be available). Furthermore, the statistical power of any test is limited by a small sample size. (A greater amount of variance will be attributed to error in smaller sample sizes, reducing the chances of a significant finding.) A value known as Box's M, given by most statistical programs, can be examined to determine whether the sample size is too small. Box's M determines whether the covariance in different groups is significantly different and must not be significant if one wishes to demonstrate that the sample sizes in each cell are adequate. An alternative is Levene's test of homogeneity of variance which tolerates violations of normality better than Box's M. However, rather than directly testing the size of the sample it examines whether the amount of variance is equally represented within the independent variable groups.

In complex MANOVA models the likelihood of achieving robust analysis is intrinsically linked to the sample size. There are restrictions associated with the generalisability of the results when the sample size is small and therefore researchers should be encouraged to obtain as large a sample as possible.

EXAMPLE OF MANOVA

Considering an example may help to illustrate the difference between ANOVAs and MANOVAs. Kaufman and McLean (1998) used a questionnaire to investigate the relationship between interests and intelligence. They used the Kaufman Adolescent and Adult Intelligence Test (KAIT) and the Strong Interest Inventory (SII) which contained six subscales on occupational themes (GOT) and 23 Basic Interest Scales (BISs). They used a MANOVA model which had four independent

Table 2.1 The different aspects of the data considered by the MANOVA model used by Kaufman and McLean (1998)

Level	Independent variables	6 GOT subscales	23 BISS subscales
Main effects	Age		Sig.
	Gender	Sig.	Sig.
	KAIT IQ	Sig.	Sig.
	F-C		
Two-way interactions	Age × Gender	Sig.	Sig.
	Age × KAIT IQ		
	Age × F-C		
	Gender × KAIT IQ		
	Gender × F-C		
	KAIT IQ × F-C		
Three-way interactions	Age × Gender × KAIT IQ		
	Age × Gender × F-C		
	Age × KAIT IQ × F-C		
	Gender × KAIT IQ × F-C		
	Age KAIT IQ × F-C		
Four-way interactions	Age × Gender × KAIT IQ × F-C		

variables: age, gender, KAIT IQ and Fluid-Crystal intelligence (F-C). The dependent variables were the six occupational theme subscales (GOT) and the twenty-three Basic Interest Scales (BISs).

In Table 2.1 the dependent variables are listed in the third and fourth columns. The independent variables are listed in the second column, with the increasingly complex interactions being shown below the main variables.

If an ANOVA had been used to examine this data, each of the GOT and BIS subscales would have been placed in a separate ANOVA. However, since the GOT and BIS scales are related, the results from separate ANOVAs would not be independent. Using multiple ANOVAs would increase the risk of a Type I error (a significant finding which occurs by chance due to repeating the same test a number of times).

Kaufman and McLean used the Wilks' lambda multivariate statistic (similar to the F values in univariate analysis) to consider the significance of their results and reported only the interactions which were significant. These are shown as Sig. in Table 2.1. The values which proved to be significant are the majority of the main effects and one of the two-way interactions. Note that although KAIT IQ had a significant main effect, none of the interactions which included this variable were significant. On the other hand, Age and Gender show a significant interaction in the effect which they have on the dependent variables.

What a MANOVA does

Like an ANOVA, MANOVA examines the degree of variance within the independent variables and determines whether it is smaller than the degree of variance between the independent variables. If the within-subjects variance is smaller than the between-subjects variance it means the independent variable has had a significant effect on the dependent variables. There are two main differences between MANOVAs and ANOVAs. The first is that MANOVAs are able to take into account multiple independent and multiple dependent variables within the same model, permitting greater complexity. Second, rather than using the F value as the indicator of significance a number of multivariate measures (Wilks' lambda, Pillai's trace, Hotelling's trace and Roy's largest root) are used. (An explanation of these multivariate statistics is given below.)

MANOVA deals with the multiple dependent variables by combining them in a linear manner to produce a combination which best separates the independent variable groups. An ANOVA is then performed on the newly developed dependent variable. In MANOVAs the independent variables relevant to each main effect are weighted to give them priority in the calculations performed. In interactions the independent variables are equally weighted to determine whether or not they have an additive effect in terms of the combined variance they account for in the dependent variable(s).

The main effects of the independent variables and of the interactions are examined with 'all else held constant'. The effect of each of the independent variables is tested separately. Any multiple interactions are tested separately from one another and from any significant main effects. Assuming there are equal sample sizes both in the main effects and the interactions, each test performed will be independent of the next or previous calculation (except for the error term which is calculated across the independent variables).

There are two aspects of MANOVAs which are left to researchers: first, they decide which variables are placed in the MANOVA. Variables are included in order to address a particular research question or hypothesis, and the best combination of dependent variables is one in which they are not correlated with one another, as explained above. Second, the researcher has to interpret a significant result. A statistical main effect of an independent variable implies that the independent variable groups are significantly different in terms of their scores on the dependent variable. (But this does not establish that the independent variable has caused the changes in the dependent variable. In a study which was poorly designed, differences in dependent variable scores may be the result of extraneous, uncontrolled or confounding variables.)

To tease out higher level interactions in MANOVA, smaller ANOVA models which include only the independent variables which were significant can be used in separate analyses and followed by *post hoc* tests. *Post hoc* and preplanned comparisons compare all the possible paired combinations of the independent variable groups. For example, for three ethnic groups of white, African and Asian the comparisons would be: white v African, white v Asian, African v Asian. The most frequently used preplanned and *post hoc* tests are least squares difference (LSD), Scheffé, Bonferroni and Tukey. The tests will give the mean difference between each group and a *p* value to indicate whether the two groups differ significantly.

The *post hoc* and preplanned tests differ from one another in how they calculate the *p* value for the mean difference between groups. Some are more conservative than others. LSD performs a series of *t* tests only after the null hypothesis (that there is no overall difference between the three groups) has been rejected. It is the most liberal of the *post hoc* tests and has a high Type I error rate. The Scheffé test uses the *F* distribution rather than the *t* distribution of the LSD tests and is considered more conservative. It has a high Type II error rate but is considered appropriate when there are a large number of groups to be compared. The Bonferroni approach uses a series of *t* tests but corrects the significance level for multiple testing by dividing the significance levels by the number of tests being performed (for the example given above this would be 0.05/3). Since this test corrects for the number of comparisons being performed, it is generally used when the number of groups to be compared is small. Tukey's honesty significance difference test also corrects for multiple comparisons, but it considers the power of the study to detect differences between groups rather than just the number of tests being carried out; that is, it takes into account sample size as well as the number of tests being performed. This makes it preferable when there are a large number of groups being compared, since it reduces the chances of a Type I error occurring.

The statistical packages which perform MANOVAs produce many figures in their output, only some of which are of interest to the researcher.

Sum of squares

The sum of squares measure found in a MANOVA, like that reported in the ANOVA, is the measure of the squared deviations from the mean both within and between the independent variable. In MANOVA, the sums of squares are controlled for covariance between the independent variables.

There are six different methods of calculating the sum of squares. Type I, hierarchical or sequential sums of squares, is appropriate when the groups in the MANOVA are of equal sizes. Type I sum of squares provides a breakdown of the sums of squares for the whole model used in the MANOVA but it is particularly sensitive to the order in which the independent variables are placed in the model. If a variable is entered first, it is not adjusted for any of the other variables; if it is entered second, it is adjusted for one other variable (the first one entered); if it is placed third, it will be adjusted for the two other variables already entered.

Type II, the partially sequential sum of squares, has the advantage over Type I in that it is not affected by the order in which the variables are entered. It displays the sum of squares after controlling for the effect of other main effects and interactions but is only robust where there are even numbers of participants in each group.

Type III sum of squares can be used in models where there are uneven group sizes, although there needs to be at least one participant in each cell. It calculates the sum of squares after the independent variables have all been adjusted for the inclusion of all other independent variables in the model.

Type IV sum of squares can be used when there are empty cells in the model but it is generally thought more suitable to use Type III sum of squares under these conditions since Type IV is not thought to be good at testing lower order effects.

Type V has been developed for use where there are cells with missing data. It has been designed to examine the effects according to the degrees of freedom which are available and if the degrees of freedom fall below a given level these effects are not taken into account. The cells which remain in the model have at least the degrees of freedom that the full model would have without any cells being excluded. For those cells which remain in the model the Type III sum of squares is calculated. However, the Type V sum of squares is sensitive to the order in which the independent variables are placed in the model and the order in which they are entered will determine which cells are excluded.

Type VI sum of squares is used for testing hypotheses where the independent variables are coded using negative and positive signs, for example $+1 = $ male, $-1 = $ female.

Type III sum of squares is the most frequently used as it has the advantages of Types IV, V and VI without the corresponding restrictions.

Mean squares

The mean square is the sum of squares divided by the appropriate degrees of freedom.

Multivariate measures

In most of the statistical programs used to calculate MANOVAs there are four multivariate measures: Wilks' lambda, Pillai's trace, Hotelling–Lawley trace and Roy's largest root. The difference between the four measures is the way in which they combine the dependent variables in order to examine the amount of variance in the data. Wilks' lambda demonstrates the amount of variance accounted for in the dependent variable by the independent variable; the smaller the value, the larger the difference between the groups being analysed. One minus Wilks' lambda indicates the amount of variance in the dependent variables accounted for by the independent variables. Pillai's trace is considered the most reliable of the multivariate measures and offers the greatest protection against Type I errors with small sample sizes. Pillai's trace is the sum of the variance which can be explained by the calculation of discriminant variables. It calculates the amount of variance in the dependent variable which is accounted for by the greatest separation of the independent variables. The Hotelling–Lawley trace is generally converted to Hotelling's T-square. Hotelling's T is used when the independent variable forms two groups and represents the most significant linear combination of the dependent variables. Roy's largest root, also known as Roy's largest eigenvalue, is calculated in a similar fashion to Pillai's trace except it only considers the largest eigenvalue (i.e. the largest loading onto a vector). As the sample sizes increase the values produced by Pillai's trace, Hotelling–Lawley trace and Roy's largest root become similar. As you may be able to tell from these very broad explanations, Wilks' lambda is the easiest to understand and therefore the most frequently used measure.

Multivariate F value

This is similar to the univariate F value in that it is representative of the degree of difference in the dependent variable created by the independent variable. However, as well as being based on the sum of squares (as in ANOVA) the calculation for F used in MANOVAs also takes into account the covariance of the variables.

EXAMPLE OF OUTPUT OF SPSS

The data analysed in this example came from a large-scale study with three dependent variables which were thought to measure distinct aspects of behaviour. The first was total score on the Dissociative Experiences Scale, the second was reaction time when completing a signal detection task, and the third was a measure of people's hallucinatory experiences (the Launay Slade Hallucinations Scale, LSHS). The independent variable was the degree to which participants were considered prone to psychotic experiences (labelled PRONE in the output shown in Figure 2.1), divided into High, Mean and Low.

The first part of the output is shown in Figure 2.1. The Between-Subjects Factors table displays the independent variable levels. Here there is only one independent variable with three levels. The number of participants in each of the independent variable groups is displayed in the column on the far right.

The Multivariate Tests table displays the multivariate values: Pillai's Trace, Wilks' Lambda, Hotelling's Trace and Roy's Largest Root. These are the multivariate values for the model as a whole. The F values for the intercept, shown in the first part of the table, are all the same. Those for the independent variable labelled PRONE are all different, but they are all significant above the 1% level (shown by Sig. being .000), indicating that on the dependent variables there is a significant difference between the three proneness groups.

General Linear Model

Between-Subjects Factors

		Value Label	N
Psychosis proneness	1.00	High	26
	2.00	Mean	12
	3.00	Low	13

Multivariate Tests[c]

Effect		Value	F	Hypothesis df	Error df	Sig.
Intercept	Pillai's Trace	.983	913.387[a]	3.000	46.000	.000
	Wilks' Lambda	.017	913.387[a]	3.000	46.000	.000
	Hotelling's Trace	59.569	913.387[a]	3.000	46.000	.000
	Roy's Largest Root	59.569	913.387[a]	3.000	46.000	.000
PRONE	Pillai's Trace	.467	4.775	6.000	94.000	.000
	Wilks' Lambda	.537	5.593[a]	6.000	92.000	.000
	Hotelling's Trace	.855	6.412	6.000	90.000	.000
	Roy's Largest Root	.846	13.254[b]	3.000	47.000	.000

a. Exact statistic
b. The statistic is an upper bound on F that yields a lower bound on the significance level
c. Design: Intercept + PRONE

Tests of Between-Subjects Effects

Source	Dependent Variable	Type III Sum of Squares	df	Mean Square	F	Sig.
Corrected Model	Dissociative Experiences Scale (DES)	18.824[a]	2	9.412	4.866	.012
	Total mean reaction time	.014[b]	2	.007	2.584	.086
	Launay Slade Hallucinations Scale	149.836[c]	2	74.918	14.366	.000
Intercept	Dissociative Experiences Scale (DES)	481.547	1	481.547	248.965	.000
	Total mean reaction time	.539	1	.539	196.171	.000
	Launay Slade Hallucinations Scale	10318.465	1	10318.465	1978.609	.000
PRONE	Dissociative Experiences Scale (DES)	18.824	2	9.412	4.866	.012
	Total mean reaction time	.014	2	.007	2.584	.086
	Launay Slade Hallucinations Scale	149.836	2	74.918	14.366	.000

Continued

Source	Dependent Variable	Type III Sum of Squares	df	Mean Square	F	Sig.
Error	Dissociative Experiences Scale (DES)	92.841	48	1.934		
	Total mean reaction time	.132	48	.003		
	Launay Slade Hallucinations Scale	250.321	48	5.215		
Total	Dissociative Experiences Scale (DES)	721.464	51			
	Total mean reaction time	.804	51			
	Launay Slade Hallucinations Scale	12824.000	51			
Corrected Total	Dissociative Experiences Scale (DES)	111.665	50			
	Total mean reaction time	.146	50			
	Launay Slade Hallucinations Scale	400.157	50			

a. R Squared = .169 (Adjusted R Squared = .134)
b. R Squared = .097 (Adjusted R Squared = .060)
c. R Squared = .374 (Adjusted R Squared = .348)

Figure 2.1   Example of main output from SPSS for MANOVA

The Tests of Between-Subjects Effects table gives the sum of squares, degrees of freedom, mean square value, the *F* values and the significance levels for each dependent variable. (The Corrected Model is the variance in the dependent variables which the independent variables accounts for without the intercept being taken into consideration.) The section of the table which is of interest is where the source under consideration is the independent variable, the row for PRONE. In this row it can be seen that two (DES, Launay Slade Hallucinations Scale) out of the three dependent variables included in the model are significant ($p < .05$), meaning that three proneness groups differ significantly in their scores on the DES and the LSHS.

To determine which of the three independent variable groups differ from one another on the dependent variables, least squares difference comparisons were performed by selecting the relevant option in SPSS. The output is shown in Figure 2.2. The table is split into broad rows, one for each dependent variable, and within each row the three groups of high, mean or low proneness are compared one against the other. The mean differences between the two groups under consideration are given in one column and then separate columns show the standard error, significance and the lower and upper 95% confidence intervals. For the DES dependent variable, the High group is significantly different from the Low

Psychosis proneness

Multiple Comparisons

LSD

Dependent variable	(I) Psychosis proneness	(J) Psychosis proneness	Mean Difference (I–J)	Std. Error	Sig.	95% Confidence interval	
						Lower Bound	Upper Bound
Dissociative Experiences Scale (DES)	High	Mean	.8811	.48536	.076	-.0947	1.8570
		Low	1.4119*	.47242	.004	.4621	2.3618
	Mean	High	-.8811	.48536	.076	-1.8570	.0947
		Low	.5308	.55675	.345	-.5886	1.6502
	Low	High	-1.4119*	.47242	.004	-2.3618	-.4621
		Mean	-.5308	.55675	.345	-1.6502	.5886
Total mean reaction time	High	Mean	.013424	.0182939	.467	-.023359	.050206
		Low	.040478*	.0178060	.028	.004677	.076279
	Mean	High	-.013424	.0182939	.467	-.050206	.023359
		Low	.027054	.0209845	.203	-.015138	.069247
	Low	High	-.040478*	.0178060	.028	-.076279	-.004677
		Mean	-.027054	.0209845	.203	-.069247	.015138
Launay Slade Hallucinations Scale	High	Mean	1.9487*	.79697	.018	.3463	3.5511
		Low	4.1154*	.77571	.000	2.5557	5.6751
	Mean	High	-1.9487*	.79697	.018	-3.5511	-.3463
		Low	2.1667*	.91419	.022	.3286	4.0048
	Low	High	-4.1154*	.77571	.000	-5.6751	-2.5557
		Mean	-2.1667*	.91419	.022	-4.0048	-.3286

Based on observed means.
* The mean difference is significant at the .05 level.

Figure 2.2 The least squares difference output from SPSS MANOVA analysis

Report

Psychosis proneness		Dissociative Experiences Scale Total	Launay Slade Hallucinations Scale
High	Mean	19.1187	17.2258
	N	34	31
	Std. Deviation	12.66749	2.84850
Mean	Mean	13.7477	15.2000
	N	31	30
	Std. Deviation	9.00164	2.00688
Low	Mean	8.6049	13.0303
	N	32	33
	Std. Deviation	6.56371	1.04537
Total	Mean	13.9337	15.1064
	N	97	94
	Std. Deviation	10.64855	2.69794

Figure 2.3   Means for the three psychosis proneness groups on the DES and the LSHS

group ($p=0.004$) but not from the Mean group ($p=0.076$). Similarly, for the Total mean reaction time dependent variable, the High group differs significantly from the Low group but not from the Mean group. For both these dependent variables, the Mean group does not differ from the High group nor from the Low group. For the Launay scale, the High group differs significantly from the Mean and Low groups, both of which also differ from each other.

The means and standard deviations on the DES and LSHS for the three proneness groups are displayed in Figure 2.3, which was produced by SPSS. Tables such as this assist in interpreting the results.

The MANOVA above could also have included another independent variable, such as gender. The interaction between the two independent variables on the dependent variables would have been reported in the Multivariate Statistics and Tests of Between Subjects Effects tables.

EXAMPLE OF THE USE OF MANOVA

From health

Snow and Bruce (2003) explored the factors involved in Australian teenage girls smoking, collecting data from 241 participants aged between 13 and 16 years of age.

Respondents completed a number of questionnaires including an Adolescent Coping Scale. They were also asked to indicate how frequently they smoked cigarettes and the responses were used to divide the respondents into three smoking groups (current smokers, experimental smokers, never smokers). In their analysis, Snow and Bruce used MANOVA with smoking group as the independent variable. In one of the MANOVAs, the dependent variables were the measures on three different coping strategies. Snow and Bruce were only interested in the main effects of smoking group on the dependent variables so they converted Wilks' lambda to F values and significance levels. They used Scheffé *post hoc* analysis to determine which of the three smoking groups differed significantly on the dependent variables, and found that on the 'productive' coping strategy there was a significant difference between the current and experimental smokers, on the 'nonproductive' coping strategy there was a difference between the current smokers and those who had never smoked, and on the 'rely on others' coping strategy there was a difference between current and experimental smokers.

FAQs

How do I maximise the power in a MANOVA?

Power refers to the sensitivity of your study design to detect true significant findings when using statistical analysis. Power is determined by the significance level chosen, the effect size and the sample size. (There are many free programs available on the Internet which can be used to calculate effect sizes from previous studies by placing means and sample sizes into the equations.) A small effect size will need a large sample size for significant differences to be detected, while a large effect size will need a relatively small sample to be detected.

In general, the power of your analysis will increase the larger the effect size and sample size. Taking a practical approach, obtaining as large a sample as possible will maximise the power of your study.

What do I do if I have groups with uneven sample sizes?

Having unequal sample sizes can effect the integrity of the analysis. One possiblity is to recruit more participants into the groups which are under-represented in the data set, another is to delete cases randomly from the more numerous groups until they are equal to the least numerous one.

What do I do if I think there may be a covariate with the dependent variables included in a MANOVA model?

When a covariate is incorporated into a MANOVA it is usually referred to as a MANCOVA model. The 'best' covariate for inclusion in a model should be highly correlated with the dependent variables but not related to the independent variables. The dependent variables included in a MANCOVA are adjusted for their association with the covariate. Some experimenters include baseline data as a covariate to control for any individual differences in scores since even randomisation to different experimental conditions does not completely control for individual differences.

SUMMARY

MANOVA is used when there are multiple dependent variables as well as independent variables in the study. MANOVA combines the multiple dependent variables in a linear manner to produce a combination which best separates the independent variable groups. An ANOVA is then performed on the newly developed dependent variable.

GLOSSARY

Additive   the effect of the independent variables on one another when placed in a multi- or univariate analysis of variance.

Interaction   the combined effect of two or more independent variables on the dependent variables.

Main effect   the effect of one independent variable on the dependent variables, examined in isolation from all other independent variables.

Mean squares   the sum of squares expressed as a ratio of the degrees of freedom either within or between the different groups.

Sum of squares   the squared deviations from the mean within or between the groups. In MANOVA they are controlled for covariance.

Wilks' lambda   a statistic which can vary between 0 and 1 and which indicates whether the means of groups differ. A value of 1 indicates the groups have the same mean.

REFERENCES

Kaufman, A.S. and McLean, J.E. (1998). An investigation into the relationship between interests and intelligence. *Journal of Clinical Psychology*, 54, 279–295.

Snow, P.C. and Bruce, D.D. (2003). Cigarette smoking in teenage girls: exploring the role of peer reputations, self-concept and coping. *Health Education Research Theory and Practice*, 18, 439–452.

FURTHER READING

Anderson, T.W. (2003). *An Introduction to Multivariate Statistical Analysis*. New York: Wiley.

Rees, D.G. (2000). *Essential Statistics* (4th edn). London: Chapman and Hall/CRC Press.

INTERNET SOURCES

www.statsoftinc.com/textbook/
www2.chass.ncsu.edu/garson/pa765/manova.htm

3

Multiple Regression

WHAT MULTIPLE REGRESSION IS

Multiple regression is used to assess the relative influence of a number of independent (predicting) variables when they are used to predict a dependent variable. For example, you might wish to see how patient satisfaction is predicted by the length of time the patient saw the doctor, how clearly the doctor diagnosed the condition as rated by the patient, the patient's sex, age, complexity of medical history, etc. Multiple regression reveals which of these variables predicts patient satisfaction and which are more important in making the prediction.

WHEN DO YOU NEED MULTIPLE REGRESSION?

Multiple regression is needed when you have a measure of an output or predicted variable which has been measured on a continuous scale, and measures on two or more predicting or independent variables, and you want to find out which of the independent variables predict the output variable and how much influence each one has on the prediction.

Multiple regression is used to answer three types of question:

1 What is the relative importance of the predictor variables included in the analysis? If patient satisfaction is predicted both by the time a doctor spends talking to the patient and by the clarity with which the diagnosis is explained, which of the two is the more important predictor?
2 A related question is to ask whether a particular variable adds to the accuracy of a prediction. If patient satisfaction is predicted by consultation duration and diagnostic clarity, can one make an even better prediction if one includes the patient's age in the equation?
3 Given two alternative sets of predictors, which one is the more effective? Can one predict patient satisfaction better from features of the patient (age, sex,

health history) or from features of the doctor's practice (size, distance from the patient's home, number of doctors)?

Multiple regression has been an extremely popular method of data analysis over the last 20 years because it offers the possibility of determining how important various predictors are. In education, you might be interested in investigating the relative importance of school size, family size, financial position on school attainment. Health investigators might be interested in knowing what variables predict drug consumption or which features of a hospital predict its success at treating illnesses. In management and business, one might want to know which variables influence people's job satisfaction or predict the profitability of a firm.

WORDS OF WARNING

However, some words of warning are needed. First, multiple regression will only tell you the relative importance of the predictors which have been included in the analysis. Let us assume that patient satisfaction with a doctor's service is strongly influenced by the duration of the consultation with the doctor and with the clarity of the diagnosis provided. If we are studying patient satisfaction but do not include duration of consultation in the set of predictor variables, then obviously it cannot show up as a strong predictor. So multiple regression cannot show what are the important predictors, only the relative strength of the predictors included in the analysis. It is up to the investigator to decide on the variables to include.

Second, multiple regression tells you the relative importance of the predictors for the respondents who provided the data. But this does not mean that these predictors will have the same relative importance for a different group of respondents. One hopes that if consultation length and clarity of diagnosis predict patient satisfaction in Scotland, they will also do so in Germany. The question of whether predictors behave consistently on a fresh data set is known as cross-validation.

Third, correlation does not establish causation: knowing that consultation length predicts patient satisfaction does not show that it causes patient satisfaction. (It is possible that a more sympathetic doctor spends longer in consultation and pleases the patient by the manner the doctor adopts, so that the link between satisfaction and consultation length is because both are a consequence of the doctor's manner.)

RECAPITULATION OF CORRELATION AND REGRESSION

As you will know, the degree of relationship between two continuous variables is expressed in terms of a correlation coefficient which can vary from -1.00 through 0 to $+1.00$. A negative correlation occurs when an increase in one variable is

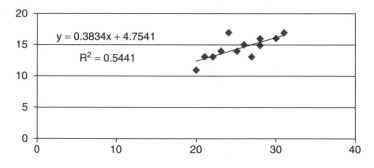

Figure 3.1 Example of a scattergram

associated with a decrease in another: for example, the number of people flying the Atlantic goes up as the price of an air ticket goes down. A positive correlation is when an increase in one variable is associated with an increase in another, for example the larger a person's foot, the taller they are.

The relationship between two variables is shown graphically in a scattergram like that shown in Figure 3.1. The closer the points are to forming a straight line, the higher the correlation. The straight line which provides the best fit to the points in the scattergram can be found and it represents visually the regression equation which looks like this:

$$y = a + b(x)$$

In the equation, y is the predicted score on the dependent variable, which is plotted on the vertical axis, and x is the score on the independent variable, which is plotted on the horizontal; a is the intercept, the point at which the line crosses the y axis. (It is the value of y when x is zero. It may be quite hypothetical in that one cannot have a value of $x = 0$. For example, one might plot foot size against height, but one could not have a foot size of 0.) In the regression equation, b is the regression coefficient and tells you by how much you must multiply x to obtain the predicted value of y. For example, the regression equation for the data shown in Figure 3.1 is $4.75 + 0.38x$. So if someone had a score of 25 on x, the predicted value of y is $4.75 + (0.38$ multiplied by $25) = 14.25$. You will see if you look at the graph that someone who had a score of 25 on x actually obtained a score of 14 on y. This difference between the predicted y score and the actual one is known as the residual: here it is $14.25 - 14.00 = 0.25$.

RECAPITULATION OF PARTIAL CORRELATION

Suppose in an investigation of patient satisfaction we have obtained from a number of respondents measures on three variables: their level of satisfaction, the length of the consultation they had and their estimate of the clarity of the diagnosis they received. We might expect that satisfaction is related to consultation length, with longer consultations being associated with higher satisfaction, and that satisfaction is also related to diagnostic clarity, with more satisfaction among patients who felt they had a clearer diagnosis. Assume we find the correlations shown in this table:

	Patient satisfaction	Consultation length	Diagnostic clarity
Patient satisfaction	1.00	0.61	0.71
Consultation length		1.00	0.34
Diagnostic clarity			1.00

The entries in the table show that consultation length and diagnostic clarity both correlate with satisfaction (0.61 and 0.71 respectively), and that consultation length and diagnostic clarity are themselves correlated 0.34. So perhaps the relationship between satisfaction and consultation length arises because longer consultations tend to contain clearer diagnoses and it is this relationship which leads to the apparent link between satisfaction and consultation length. To find out if this is the case, we would want to look at the relationship between satisfaction and consultation length when the influence of diagnostic clarity had been removed or, to use the appropriate jargon, partialled out. This is achieved by calculating the partial correlation coefficient.

For the data summarised in the table above, the partial correlation between satisfaction and consultation length with diagnostic clarity partialled out is 0.57, a little lower than the 0.61 in the table. But since it is still substantial (at 0.57), the relationship is not solely due to longer consultations having clearer diagnoses included in them. (You cannot work out the partial correlation from the data in the table: it has been calculated from the figures which generated the correlation coefficients.) So a partial correlation is when the correlation between two variables has been calculated and the effect of a correlation between one of the variables and a third variable has been removed.

In multiple regression, the effects of each independent variable are found when the others have been partialled out. So in multiple regression, the correlation of each independent variable with the dependent variable is the correlation when the effect of the other independent variables has been removed.

THE REGRESSION EQUATION IN MULTIPLE REGRESSION

Multiple regression is an extension of simple regression in that it has more than one predictor. Although you can predict height from footsize, you may be able to get a more accurate estimate if you predicted it from footsize and the person's weight. So in multiple regression one uses two or more predictors to predict the score on the dependent variable. The usual aim of multiple regression is not in fact to predict the dependent variable (because you have already collected scores on it) but to see which variables do predict it and which ones have most influence on the prediction. So you might ask whether predicting height from footsize and weight is better than predicting it only from footsize, and if so which of the predictors has most influence on making a successful prediction.

In multiple regression, the regression equation becomes:

$$Y = a + B_1(x_1) + B_2(x_2) + \cdots + B_K(x_K)$$

Multiple regression aims to find the regression coefficients or weights (B_1, B_2, etc.) for each of the predictor variables (x_1, x_2, etc.) which will give the values of y which are closest to the actual values. So the weights are chosen which reduce to a minimum the differences between the predicted values of y and the actual values, the residuals. (They actually reduce the sum of the squared differences between the predicted and actual y values.) This means the correlation between the combination of the predictor values and the predicted y values will be maximised.

For each predictor, the regression weight, B, is the amount of change in the dependent variable resulting from a one-unit change in the independent variable when all other independent variables are held constant. However, the size of B is related to the scale used to measure the independent variable; if you were using monthly income as an independent variable, the regression weight obtained when you measure income in pounds would not be the same as the one obtained when you measured it in hundreds of pounds. You use B when making a prediction from a person's score or measure on an independent variable, but to compare the influence of different independent variables you need to have them based on a common scale. This is achieved by looking at the standardised coefficients or beta values. These can vary from −1 to +1.

In simple regression, r is the correlation between the independent and the dependent variables. r^2 shows how much of the variance in the dependent variable is accounted for (explained by) the variance in the independent variable. So if the correlation is 0.7, then 0.49 or 49% of the variance in the dependent variable is explained by the independent variable. Multiple regression works in a similar fashion. The multiple regression equation expresses the relationship between the predicted variable and the set of predictor variables as a correlation coefficient R. R^2 is the proportion of the variance in the predicted variable which is accounted for by the best linear combination of the predictors. So if two independent variables have a multiple correlation with the dependent variable of 0.8, $R^2 = 0.64$ and they are explaining 0.64 or 64% of the variance in the dependent variable. R^2 is the most useful indicator of how effective the prediction is.

WHAT KINDS OF DATA ARE NEEDED?

You start a multiple regression study by collecting a number of items of information on each case. In psychology, a 'case' is most likely to be a person. For example, you might collect data from a number of respondents on their satisfaction with the medical consultation they have received, the length of time they saw the doctor, how clearly the doctor diagnosed their condition as rated by the patient, the patient's sex, age, complexity of medical history. In other disciplines a case might be a much broader entity. For example, one might wish to look at predicting countries' gross domestic product from national characteristics such as population size, climate, level of industrialisation. Here, each 'case' would be a country.

The predicted (dependent) variable needs to be measured on a continuous numerical scale. The predictor (independent) variables can be continuous, categorical or a mixture of the two. An example of a continuous variable is age, which can vary continuously from a few minutes to 100 years or more. A categorical variable is one which divides cases into classes; if you separated your respondents into age groups such as 1 for 0–20 years, 2 for 21–40, 3 for 41 and above, then you would have transformed your age data into a categorical variable. But age groups form an ordered scale, with the numbers representing a quantitative feature: 21–40 is greater than 0–20. Such a scale can be used in multiple regression. If you are using a categorical scale which is not ordered (a nominal scale), then in multiple regression the variable has to have only two values. Sex is an obvious example: you might code male as 1 and female as 2; this is not an ordered scale since the size of the numbers means nothing – you could just as easily coded male as 2 and female as 1. Here is another example: Ali and Davies (2003) used multiple regression in a study of the productivity of Malaysian rubber tappers. One of their independent variables was tenure – how long the worker had been doing the job; this is a continuous variable. Another variable was the terrain of the rubber plantation; as this is a nominal scale, they divided terrain into two types, hilly or undulating. Nominal (non-ordered) category scales in multiple regression must only have two categories, since a two-category scale has a linear relationship with other variables and multiple regression assumes linear relationships. A nominal category scale with more than two categories can have a non-linear relationship with other variables.

HOW MUCH DATA? (HOW MANY RESPONDENTS FOR HOW MANY INDEPENDENT VARIABLES?)

Authorities differ in what they consider to be the minimum number of respondents needed for a multiple regression analysis. Some recommend 15 times as many respondents as independent variables and Howell (2002) notes that others have suggested that N should be at least $40 + k$ (where k is the number of independent variables). Tabachnick and Fidell (1996) cite other authorities in recommending that N should be at least $50 + 8k$ for testing multiple correlation and at least $104 + k$ for testing individual predictors. If in doubt, they suggest, calculate N both ways and use the larger figure.

WHICH INDEPENDENT VARIABLES TO INCLUDE?

As we have noted, the result of multiple regression depends on the variables included. Which ones to include should be based on theoretical considerations: select variables which you expect, perhaps from previous research, to be predictive and which are not too highly correlated with each other. For practical reasons, it is wise to select variables where it is not too difficult or expensive to obtain the data.

TECHNICAL CONSIDERATIONS AND SCREENING THE DATA

Before doing the multiple regression analysis, you should examine your data to see if there are outliers, scores which are very different from the other scores on that variable. You should also see how far the independent variables are correlated with each other, a topic known as multicollinearity. You can also discover whether the data meets the requirements of being normally distributed, linearly related and homoscedastic (a term explained below).

OUTLIERS

Outliers are items of data which are deviant, a long way from the mean. For example, if you were measuring people's height a measurement of 200 cm (almost 6 ft 7 in) would be an outlier since very few people are that tall. Outliers can occur from simply making a mistake when entering the data – you might have keyed in 1000 when you meant 100. Such errors obviously need to be corrected to ensure one is analysing accurate data. So the first stage in screening the data is to look at the scores and check the accuracy of any aberrant ones. But you may (and often do) have genuine aberrant scores – you may really have a respondent who is 200 cm tall.

Outliers can have a considerable impact on the results of multiple regression, and the impact is expressed in terms of leverage and discrepancy which together determine influence. Leverage means the case is distant from the others but basically on the same trend line. Discrepancy is the extent to which the case is out of line with the other cases. Influence is assessed by determining the amount a regression coefficient changes when the outlier is deleted from the analysis. It is expressed in a measure known as Cook's distance, and if this is greater than 1 the case is an outlier.

If you have outliers with a high influence, what should you do? One option – and the simplest – is to remove them from the analysis. Alternatively, you can transform the variable or rescore the outlier. There are a number of ways of transforming the data on a variable to make its distribution closer to a normal one; the square root transformation may do this. You take the square root of each score on that particular variable and check that the transformed (square root) scores form a normal distribution. The problem with using transformed scores is that they are more difficult to understand: you might be able to interpret a correlation between educational achievement and family income, but be at a bit of a loss if the relationship is between educational achievement and the square root of income!

One way to rescore a variable to eliminate outliers is to give the outlier(s) one scale unit more extreme than the next most extreme score. For example, suppose you have measured income on this scale expecting this will cover all your respondents: 1 means less than 10,000; 2 represents 10,000–19,999; 3 represents 20,000–29,999; 4 represents 30,000–39,999; 5 represents 40,000–49,999; 6 represents 50,000–59,999. But you then find someone who reports their income to be 1,000,000. Rather than extending your original scale to include this figure, you would just give this value a score of 7.

Any outliers on any of the variables can be identified just by looking at graphical plots of the distribution of those scores. But multiple regression is concerned with looking at the effects of multiple variables, and it is possible to have cases which are outliers from the aggregated variables. Whether or not a case is an outlier is shown by the value of Mahalanobis distance (which expresses the distance of the case from the mean of all the variables). If you are using SPSS, you can obtain this statistic by selecting the Save button in the window which opens when you select Regression and then Linear from the Analyze menu. (The significance of the statistic has to be discovered by finding a value of chi-square with degrees of freedom equal to the number of variables included in the analysis and applying a significance level of 0.001. This is likely to be a matter beyond the level of interest of most students.)

MULTICOLLINEARITY

Multicollinearity means that the predictor variables are themselves correlated to an undesirable degree – which immediately prompts the questions 'why does it matter?' and 'what is an undesirable level?'

Suppose that patient satisfaction is correlated with consultation duration and diagnostic clarity – each of these can predict satisfaction on their own. But if the two predictors are themselves correlated, one does not know which of them is explaining the variance in the dependent variable. So you are left with an ambiguous outcome.

Multicollinearity is shown by low tolerance: a tolerance value of 1 indicates that a variable is not correlated with others, and a value of 0 one that is perfectly correlated. There is also another index: VIF, which stands for Variance Inflation Factor. A value of 2 for VIF shows a close correlation, and a value of 1 shows little correlation. So both tolerance and VIF should be in the region of 1. (In SPSS you can find the tolerance and VIF figures if you select the Statistics button in the Analyze | Regression | Linear window and check the box for Collinearity diagnostics.)

If there is multicollinearity, one answer is to remove one of the variables which has a low value on tolerance and rerun the analysis. Alternatively, you can combine correlated independent variables by perhaps using their total or mean as an independent variable. (This should only be attempted if combining the variables makes logical sense.)

NORMALLY DISTRIBUTED, LINEARLY RELATED, HOMOSCEDASTIC?

Multiple regression assumes that the scores on the variables are normally distributed, linear and homoscedastic. This last term means the variance of the dependent variable does not differ at different levels of the independent variable. One way of determining whether the dependent variable is normally distributed is to look at the plot of the distribution of scores on each variable. To check all three assumptions, one can study plots of the residuals, the differences between the scores predicted by the multiple regression equation and the actual scores. They can be examined to see if they are normally distributed (they should be), linear (they should be this too) and show an equal amount of variation at different levels of the independent variable. (The opposite of homoscedasticity is heteroscedasticity, and is something one does not want.) If all three assumptions are met, the plot of the residuals against predicted scores will be roughly rectangular. If the residuals are not linear and not homoscedastic, the multiple regression is weakened. (It is similar to the situation in the common correlation calculations: if the relationship between two variables is curvilinear, you can still find the linear Pearson correlation coefficient but it will be less than it would be if the relationship were linear.)

If you are using SPSS, you can examine whether the residuals have the correct features by asking for a plot of the dependent variable scores against ZRESID (the residuals expressed as standard or z scores). (This is obtained from the Plots button in the Regression | Linear window.) The points on the scatterplot should 'reveal a pileup of residuals in the centre of the plot at each value of the predicted score and a normal distribution of residuals trailing off symmetrically from the centre' (Tabachnick and Fidell, 1996, p. 137). If you feel that the plot shows the assumptions are not met, and need to do something about it, you can transform the variables or use a weighted least squares regression. We suspect that most readers who have got this far will not want to know about how to follow these recommendations, but if you do then you need to consult one of the advanced texts.

HOW DO YOU DO MULTIPLE REGRESSION?

The obvious initial answer to this question is 'by telling the computer package to do it'. But you have to make some decisions about what instructions you are going to give the computer. The outcome of multiple regression depends not only on the variables which are included in it, but also on the particular strategy one tells the statistical package to use in entering the variables into the regression equation. There are three major alternatives. One is to instruct the program to enter all the independent (predictor) variables together at the start. This is known as simultaneous entry and in SPSS is called the Enter method. The weight for each predictor is calculated as though that variable were the last one entered into the equation and if it adds to the power of the prediction, the variable is retained; if not it is removed from the equation.

An alternative procedure is the hierarchical or sequential method, where variables are entered into the equation in an order specified by the investigator. Each one is evaluated to see if it adds to the prediction, given that the other previously entered variables are already in the equation. If it does not add to the prediction, it is not kept in the equation. This procedure requires the investigator to decide on the order in which the variables are entered, and this needs to be guided by some reasonable theoretical expectation.

The third procedure, statistical regression, is where the program decides on statistical grounds which variables to enter and in which order. There are variations even here, as one can have all the variables entered and then remove those which do not add to the equation removed (backward selection) or one can have the equation empty to start with and variables entered one at a time and kept in whatever happens later (forward selection). A third alternative (stepwise) is a compromise in which the variables are added but can subsequently be removed if they no longer contribute to the prediction. Statistical regression may appear attractive since it leaves the program to decide which variables are entered, which retained and which removed and this may seem to be an impartial way of making these decisions. But the authorities look disapprovingly on the use of stepwise because the statistical differences on which decisions are made may be very small and can produce misleading outcomes, and the procedure ignores any theoretical justification for including some variables rather than others.

So the procedures differ in the order in which they enter and evaluate the value of the independent variables. You might ask why the order is important. Put simply, there is variance in the dependent variable to be explained. If independent variable number 1 is entered into the equation and explains 50% of the variance in the dependent variable, then there is only the remaining 50% available for independent variable number 2 to explain. So there is a limit on how much variance it can explain. But if the second independent variable were entered first, it has potentially 100% of the dependent variable which it can explain.

Note that when considering which procedure to employ, the experts (Tabachnick and Fidell, 1996, p. 153) assert 'To simply assess relationships among variables, and answer the basic question of multiple correlation, the method of choice is standard multiple regression. Reasons for using sequential regression are theoretical or for testing explicit hypotheses.'

When you have decided the procedure to apply, you then have to interpret the output and decide what it is telling you. Here it is important to appreciate what R^2 means. R^2 is the proportion of the variance in the dependent variable which is accounted for by the predictor variables included in the model being tested. Using the Enter procedure, there is only one R^2 value because all the variables are entered and their strengths are calculated. But in hierarchical or stepwise regression, one independent variable is entered into the equation and R and R^2 are calculated. Then another independent variable is entered, and R and R^2 for the two independent variables together are calculated. The difference between the first R^2 with one independent variable and the second R^2 with two independent variables is calculated, and is the change in R^2. The size of this change is evaluated, and if it is sufficiently large the second variable is kept in the equation. If the change in R^2 is not sufficiently large, the second variable is dropped. This process is then repeated for all the other independent variables. So at the end of the process one is left with an equation which contains those independent variables which have added to the prediction and been retained in the equation, with the regression coefficient for each one. The output provides a series of R^2 values and shows how R^2 has changed at each step.

The value of R^2, the coefficient of determination, is calculated on the set of data being analysed. One hopes that the results of the analysis will apply to the wider population from which the set of data was drawn. But the R^2 calculated from the sample will be an overestimate of the R^2 which would be obtained from the wider population, and to obtain a more accurate estimate of what the value would be on that wider population one has to make a correction which allows for the number of respondents and the number of predictor variables. The value of R^2 after that correction has been made is an adjusted R^2 which is shown in the output (and is always less than the original R^2).

CROSS-VALIDATION

Multiple regression finds a solution, a regression equation, for the data used in the analysis. But one hopes the results generalise to other sets of data. Whether they do or not is the issue of cross-validation. The best way of testing for cross-validation is to obtain data on a fresh sample of respondents, and see if multiple regression produces a similar outcome. Another approach is to divide the sample you have and test the multiple regression model on the two halves to see if one obtains a similar outcome. One assesses 'similar' by using the hierarchical method to insert variables in the equation in a specified order and comparing the R^2 values. They should be similar.

INTERACTIONS

Interaction means that the effect of one variable differs according to the level on another variable. For example, most people are happier if they have more money (up to a certain point at which happiness levels off). But this is probably only true if one has good health: if one's health is poor, more money does not make one happier. How can one investigate such interactions in a multiple regression analysis?

Using this example, we might predict that scores on some scale of 'happiness' are predicted by income and by healthiness and by an interaction between income and healthiness. An interaction in multiple regression is referred to by Howell (2002) as a moderating relationship. He describes the steps needed to see whether the interaction is a predictor of the scores on the dependent variable. First, one should 'centre' the data on the two independent variables, meaning that for each independent variable one takes each score and subtracts from it the mean of the scores on that variable. So anyone whose score is at the mean will have a centred score of 0. Second, the centred scores on each of the two independent variables are multiplied together to give an 'interaction' score for each respondent. Third, the centred predictors and the interaction scores are entered into a multiple regression analysis. The interaction is significant if the regression coefficient for the interaction scores is shown to be significant.

Although this procedure is not difficult, it is worth noting Howell's comment (Howell, 2002, p. 582) that 'my experience and that of others have been that it is surprisingly difficult to find meaningful situations where the regression coefficient for $X_1 \times X_2$ [the interaction between X_1 and X_2] is significant, especially in experimental settings'.

EXAMPLES OF MULTIPLE REGRESSION AND ITS INTERPRETATION

From psychology

In the field of cognitive psychology, there has been considerable interest in the speed with which people can identify pictures of objects. Bonin et al. (2002) presented respondents with over 200 drawings of objects on a computer and measured how long they took to start to name the objects either by speaking or by writing the name. They removed outliers from the data: 'latencies exceeding two standard deviations above the participant and item means were excluded' (p. 97).

Various features of the objects pictured and their names were recorded including rated image agreement (the degree to which images generated by the participants matched the picture's visual appearance), estimated age at which the respondent acquired the word (AoA, but three different measure of this were collected), rated image variability (whether the name of an object evoked few or many different images of the object), word frequency, name agreement (the degree to which participants agreed on the name of the pictured object), rated familiarity of the concept depicted, visual complexity of the drawing (the number of lines and details it contained).

Multiple regression with response latency as the dependent variable showed that the same variables had significant effects on both the oral and written response tasks. These variables were image agreement, AoA, image variability and name agreement. Other variables, including word frequency, had no effect. Bonin et al., state that 'Among the major determinants of naming onset latencies ... was the age at which the word was first learned' (p. 102) and that a noticeable finding was that word frequency 'did not emerge as a significant determinant of naming latencies' (p. 103). They conclude that their study made it possible to identify certain major determinants of spoken picture naming onset latencies. (It is noteworthy that they have nine independent variables in the table summarising the multiple regression analysis, but had only 36 respondents in each of the two tasks of spoken or written responding.)

From health

Gallagher et al. (2002) were interested in the role that women's appraisal of their breast cancer and coping resources play in psychological morbidity (high levels of anxiety or depression) at six months. From previous research, they predicted that psychosocial variables such as age under 50, having children under 21, psychiatric history and poor social support would affect morbidity but disease and treatment factors would not. They asked 195 women to fill in a number of questionnaires including (1) the General Health Questionnaire GHQ-12 which was administered after two and after six months, (2) an 'appraisal of threat' measure which allowed the women to indicate how much worry the breast cancer diagnosis had produced, (3) a measure in which they rated the coping resources available to them under the headings of self-efficacy, family support and treatment-team support, and (4) a self-report measure which identified respondents who were likely to have an affective disorder and which was used to divide the respondents into three groups: those with no symptoms, borderline cases and those with a high likelihood of affective disorder. In addition, data on psychosocial variables such as age, number of children under 21, psychiatric history was collected and used to divide the women into risk and no-risk groups. Medical information such as type of surgery and grade of tumour was also collected.

Multiple regression was used 'to enable the best explanatory model of psychological functioning at 6 months'. Appraisal ('How much of a worry is the breast cancer') and emotional support (confidence in self-efficacy, in family support) were used as independent variables and showed a significant relationship with GHQ scores at six months when GHQ score at two months was held constant. The two-month GHQ score was forced into the regression equation, and other variables entered using the stepwise procedure. 'The final model ... retained questions 1 (threat appraisal) and 2 (self-efficacy) from the appraisal questions and, in conjunction with the 2-month GHQ-12 score, accounted for 40% of the variance in psychological functioning 6 months after diagnosis' (p. 372). Grade of tumour, psychiatric history and confidence in family support were dropped because they were not significant predictors. Gallagher et al. conclude that 'the improvements in psychological functioning observed here have a stronger relationship with a woman's primary and secondary appraisals than with physical factors such as the type of treatment she receives' (p. 374).

From business/management

Ali and Davies (2003) examined the effects of age, sex and tenure on the job performance of rubber tappers in Malaysia using data from 962 respondents (415 men, 547 women) from nine rubber estates. The dependent variable was the crop obtained in 1996, measured in kilograms. The independent variables were (1) whether the estate was hilly or undulating, with hilly having a greater slope; (2) respondent age; (3) tenure on the estate where the respondents were employed, referred to as truncated tenure because it did not include tenure on any other estate: 'the regression equation obtained was total crop = $9{,}676.45 + 8.50\ X_1 +$

106.78 X_2 (where X_1 = age and X_2 = truncated tenure) … the effect of age on total crop production was not significant … while that of truncated tenure was' (p. 385). Further analysis indicated a curvilinear relationship between production and age, with a peak at age in the mid-forties, while the relationship with tenure was broadly linear. The data indicated that the women workers obtained a greater output than the men.

FAQs

What is R^2 and what does it mean?

R^2 expresses the proportion of variance in the dependent variable accounted for by the best linear combination of independent variables.

How many respondents do I need?

Count the number of predictor variables and multiply it by 8; then add 50. This gives the minimum number.

What should I do if I have too few respondents?

Collect more data from additional respondents or reduce the number of predictor variables in the analysis.

What is the difference between a regression weight and a standardised regression weight?

The regression weight, B, is the amount of change in the dependent variable resulting from a one-unit change in the independent variable when all other independent variables are held constant. The size of B depends on the scale used to measure the independent variable, so the B values for two independent variables are not comparable. To compare the influence of different independent variables, you need to use the standardised regression weights as they are all on a common scale and can vary from −1 to +1.

SUMMARY

Multiple regression assesses the relative influence of a number of independent variables when predicting a dependent variable which has been measured on a continuous numerical scale. It shows the relative importance only of the predictors which have been included in the analysis and for the respondents on whom data is available.

The outcome of multiple regression depends on the particular strategy used for entering the variables into the regression equation. There are three major alternatives, but the default preference is to enter all the independent (predictor) variables together at the start (simultaneous entry).

GLOSSARY

Cross-validation   whether predictors behave consistently on a fresh data set.

Discrepancy   the extent to which the case is out of line with the other cases.

Homoscedastic   whether the dependent variable shows an equal amount of variation at different levels of the independent variable.

Leverage   an outlier case which is distant from the others but basically on the same trend line.

Multicollinearity   when the predictor variables are themselves correlated to an undesirable degree.

Outliers   scores which are very different from the other scores on that variable.

Partial regression   the correlation between two variables when their correlation with a third variable has been removed.

R^2 the proportion of the variance in the predicted variable accounted for by the best linear combination of the predictors.

Regression weight (B)   the amount of change in the dependent variable resulting from a one-unit change in an independent variable when all other independent variables are held constant.

Sequential regression   where variables are entered into the regression equation in an order specified by the investigator.

Simultaneous entry   when all the independent (predictor) variables are entered into the regression equation together at the start.

Standardised regression weights (β)   varying from −1 to +1, they express the influence of independent variables. As they are based on a common scale, they can be used to compare the influence of different independent variables.

REFERENCES

Ali, H. and Davies, D.R. (2003). The effects of age, sex and tenure on the job performance of rubber tappers. *Journal of Occupational and Organizational Psychology*, 76, 381–391.

Bonin, P., Chalard, M., Meot, A. and Fayol, M. (2002). The determinants of spoken and written picture naming latencies. *British Journal of Psychology*, 93, 89–114.

Gallagher, J., Parle, M. and Cairns, D. (2002). Appraisal and psychological distress six months after diagnosis of breast cancer. *British Journal of Health Psychology*, 7, 365–376.

Howell, D.C. (2002). *Statistical Methods or Psychology* (5th edn). Pacific Grove, CA: Duxbury.

Tabachnick, B.G. and Fidell, L.S. (1996). *Using Multivariate Statistics* (3rd edn). New York: HarperCollins.

4

Log–linear Analysis

WHAT LOG–LINEAR ANALYSIS IS

Log–linear analysis is a multivariate statistical technique which can be applied to contingency tables for the interpretation of qualitative, categorical data. It is often used in the analysis of questionnaire data which is limited to categorical responses. Categorical data is of the sort that might be: yes/no, pre-obese/healthy, dead/alive. The frequencies of the data occurrence are compared in table form and decisions can then be made about the sorts of associations that might be present. It is the strengths of these associations that are considered in log–linear analysis.

RECAPITULATION OF CONTINGENCY TABLES

Log–linear analysis grew out of the calculations associated with contingency tables and their associated statistic, chi-square. Contingency tables organise categorical data by cross-classifying it. Suppose we had some data about 150 full-time and part-time office workers that included information about weight that was categorised as pre-obese or healthy. One way to look at this data is in a contingency table such as that shown in Table 4.1.

In Table 4.1 we can see that more full-time people have been categorised as pre-obese but we can also see that there are twice as many full-time people in the sample. If we wanted to look at the associations between work pattern (full- or part-time) and weight, we could run a chi-square analysis to determine what, if any, associations there are between variables.

Chi-square looks for associations by testing the null hypothesis that the cell frequencies are proportional to the row and column totals. (If they are, this would mean there is no relationship between the variables.)

Table 4.1 Hypothetical data on the number of people in full-time and part-time office work classified as being of healthy or pre-obese weight

	Full-time	Part-time	
Pre-obese	55	15	
Healthy	45	35	
Total	100	50	150

With chi-square you can only have two variables. If there are more, you must perform a chi-square analysis for each new variable. By the 1970s statisticians had worn out their fingers doing so many chi-square analyses and Goodman came up with a way to look at associations between two or more variables for categorical data which he called log–linear analysis. This provided a way to look at three or more variables at the same time and determine associations between them and also, critically, had the advantage over chi-square in showing just where those associations were located.

Log–linear analysis is often included in texts that look more generally at multiway frequency analysis (MFA) and indicate that log–linear analysis is an extension or part of MFA. One key aspect of the technique is already encoded in the term 'multiway frequency analysis': it is concerned with looking at frequencies, more specifically frequency or contingency tables. Frequency tables, as shown in Table 4.1, are ways of representing data that have a number of columns and rows that intersect to form cells; the cell entries are the number of cases which have the features of that particular row and column.

Many texts start out by introducing log–linear analysis as similar to ANOVA, correspondence analysis, chi-square or note that it is part of the general linear model. All these texts are correct but what they often neglect to point out is that the techniques are similar because when you perform a log–linear analysis you are looking at associations between variables (and all variables are assumed to be independent variables) and not the standard fare of looking explicitly at experimental effects. That is the essence of this type of analysis: it determines the significance of associations between variables and their interactions. In part, this has to do with the type of data (categorical) to which the analysis is applied. It also has to do with the way the data is represented: in table form. Some sources suggest log–linear analysis is simply a more sophisticated way of looking at tables or cross-tabulations.

Like many of the techniques mentioned in this book, log–linear analysis is concerned with multivariate analysis. In this case it looks at two or more categorical variables. Log–linear analysis is an inferential statistical technique, a way to make predictions about the constituents of a table and 'to see whether the cell frequencies can be adequately approximated by a model that contains fewer than the full set of treatment effects' (Kinear and Gray, 2000, p. 304).

WHEN DO YOU NEED LOG–LINEAR ANALYSIS?

There are two major characteristics of the data which lead you to use log–linear analysis. First, the data is categorical data and you wish to determine if associations between variables are present. (It may be that the data is of a continuous form, but you can always transform it into a categorical form. For example, you might have people's ages in years, but this can be turned into a categorical scale if you use age groups such as 0–19, 20–39, 40–59, etc.) The second characteristic is that you have more than two categorical variables in a contingency table. Table 4.1 has just two variables included, but Table 4.2 below has three and lends itself to log–linear analysis.

WHAT KINDS OF DATA ARE NEEDED?

The reason why we use log–linear analysis is that we have a set of frequency data and the frequencies have been subdivided into levels of three or more categorical variables. One requirement is that the data is independent, meaning that no case or respondent can appear in more than one cell of the table. So the total N must equal the number of cases. A further requirement is that the expected frequencies in the data table are sufficient. These expected frequencies should all be greater than 1 and in no more than 20% of the cells should they be less than 5. (These requirements may be familiar from previous experience with the chi-square test.)

There are no assumptions about population distributions, so there are few limitations on the data which can be used so long as the requirements noted above are met.

HOW MUCH DATA?

Tabachnik and Fiddell (1996) recommend at least five times as many cases as there are cells in the contingency table, so if you were applying log–linear analysis to the data shown in Table 4.2 below which has eight cells (because one does not count the cells in the Total rows or Total column), you would need to have data on $5 \times 8 = 40$ cases.

HOW TO DO LOG–LINEAR ANALYSIS

Lakhan and Lavalle (2002) introduce the method of log–linear analysis succinctly:

categorical data are arranged in a contingency or frequency table. Each variable in the table has a number of categories. The major emphasis of log–linear analysis is to obtain a log–linear model that is linear in the logarithms of expected frequencies of a contingency table that adequately describes or 'fits' the associations and interactions that exist in the original frequency table … . The objective is to choose a parsimonious model that adequately describes the data. (p. 77)

So log–linear analysis is a process of model development that seeks to find the model that best represents the data. This is done through goodness-of-fit tests that look at differences between the expected and the observed cell frequencies. Tabachnick and Fidell (1996) indicate that

tables are formed that contain the one-way, two-way, three-way, and higher order associations. A linear model of (the logarithm of) expected cell frequencies is developed. The log–linear model starts with all of the one-, two-, three-, and higher-way associations and then eliminates as many of them as possible while still maintaining an adequate fit between expected and observed cell frequencies. (p. 239)

These are the general steps involved and some of the terms mentioned have already been explained. Although you would use a computer program like SAS, SPSS or Statistica for Windows to perform this type of analysis, the general logic, process and terminology of log–linear analysis will be described to help you understand what it does.

In explaining how log–linear analysis operates, we shall use data from a study looking at the relationship between street crime, substance misuse and age. Popular opinion and crime statistics support the idea that drug users commit crimes to support their continued use of a drug. This study was interested particularly in street crime which can sometimes be violent and sometimes less so. The hypothesis, based on experience with long-term drug users, was that although drug users do indeed commit crimes they are rarely violent. Furthermore, it was hypothesised that the commission of street crime was related more to age than to drug use, with younger individuals being more likely to commit violent crime. The sample was 178 individuals recruited from a variety of sources including the prison and treatment services.

The first step in the analysis is to organise the data into a contingency table as shown in Table 4.2.

From this preliminary table it appears, from a simple examination of the totals, that some relationships could be present. For example, there might be a relationship between age and violent crime.

The next step is to determine if the expected cell frequencies are adequate to perform a log–linear analysis. The data in Table 4.2 has no expected frequencies less than 1 and fewer than 20% of the cells have an expected frequency less than 5,

Table 4.2 Frequency of violent and non-violent street crime offenders aged under or over 25 who did or did not exhibit substance misuse

Age			Substance misuse		
			Yes	No	Total
Under 25	Violent crime	Yes	45	42	87
		No	15	24	39
Total			60	66	126
Over 25	Violent crime	Yes	14	8	22
		No	24	6	30
Total			38	14	52

so it is acceptable to proceed with log–linear analysis. If these requirements were not met, it would be necessary to collect data on more cases, delete one of the variables or collapse categories on an appropriate variable. (This means a variable which had three categories could be reduced to two; if you had three age groups such as 0–25, 26–50, 51–75 you could reduce them to two by encoding age as 0–38 and 39+.) Alternatively, it might be possible to use a different form of analysis such as logit analysis. (The primary reason for not having frequencies less than 1 and having fewer than 20% of cells with an expected frequency less than 5 is that they substantially reduce the power of the test.)

When the log–linear analysis is run using SPSS, the observed and expected cell frequencies are the same because SPSS fits a fully saturated model to begin with. SPSS uses what is called 'backwards elimination' where it starts with the most complex model (the saturated one) and eliminates effects in a stepwise fashion. (This contrasts with 'forward addition' where the reverse occurs.) Once SPSS has performed the elimination, we are left with a parsimonious model that can still accurately represent the observed data. (The output produced by SPSS is lengthy and a good explanation of its interpretation and definitions can be found in Kinnear and Gray, 2000.) Using backwards elimination the fully saturated model is first tested. Part of the output is displayed in Figure 4.1 and shows the interaction between all variables. This interaction is shown to be nearly but not quite significant with p value ('Prob') just above the level of .05 at .0658.

In Figure 4.2, the saturated model has been pared down in a step-wise fashion so that the significant interactions remain.

In step 1 of Figure 4.2 we see the next level of elimination: in this case the relationship between misuse and violence is shown to be non-significant with $p > .05$ at .6222 and it has the smallest chi-square change (Chisq Change) at .243. Step 2 has eliminated the non-significant interaction and now compares misuse × age and violence × age. Although both are highly significant, it is violence × age that has both the lower p value and the larger chi-square change. Step 3 summarises the significant interactions.

```
            ***HIERARCHICAL LOG LINEAR***

Backward Elimination (p = .050) for DESIGN 1 with generating class

    MISUSE*VIOLENCE*AGE

Likelihood ratio chi square = .00000 DF = 0 P = 1.000

If Deleted Simple Effect is

DF        L.R. Chisq Change         Prob         Iter        MISUSE*VIOLENCE*AGE

1              3.384                 .0658          3
```

Figure 4.1 Excerpt of the output from SPSS log–linear analysis

The log–linear analysis of the data shown in Table 4.2 found that there is a relationship between substance misuse and age and one between violence and age. These are significant relationships, with the p value well below .05. But it is notable that there was no significant association between substance misuse and violence (as mentioned, p here is non-significant at .6222). So the findings are interesting compared to the original hypotheses: we thought there was a relationship between violence and age (as was found) but also predicted that substance misusers were less likely to commit violent crimes. What was demonstrated was that age is a better predictor of violent crime and that age is also related significantly to substance misuse.

Many studies use more variables than in this example. Log–linear analysis is designed to look at a number of complex relationships, but there is a limit due not so much to the technique itself but rather to the interpretation of the output: it becomes very difficult if an inordinate number of variables are included.

EXAMPLES FROM PSYCHOLOGY, HEALTH AND BUSINESS

From psychology

Lyon et al. (1997) use log–linear analysis to examine multidimensionality in anorexia. They concede that there is little doubt that the disorder has multiple causes but highlight the fact that little statistical research had been done to quantify those multiple causes. Log–linear analysis is well suited for this type of research where a number of variables need to be compared to determine which associations are most significant. For instance, it is well known through twin studies that there is a biological factor involved in anorexia but it is also known

Step 1

The best model has generating class

    MISUSE*VIOLENCE

    MISUSE*AGE

    VIOLENCE*AGE

Likelihood ratio chi square = 3.38444 DF = 1 P = .066

If Deleted Simple Effect is

DF	L.R. Chisq Change	Prob	Iter
MISUSE*VIOLENCE			
1	.243	.6222	2
MISUSE*AGE			
1	10.116	.0015	2
VIOLENCE*AGE			
1	11.070	.0009	2

Step 2

The best model has generating class

    MISUSE*AGE
    VIOLENCE*AGE

Likelihood ratio chi square = 3.62726 DF = 2 P = .163

If Deleted Simple Effect is

DF	L.R. Chisq Change	Prob	Iter
MISUSE*AGE			
1	9.971	.0016	2
VIOLENCE*AGE			
1	10.926	.0009	2

        HIERARCHICAL LOG LINEAR

Step 3

The best model has generating class

    MISUSE*AGE
    VIOLENCE*AGE

Likelihood ratio chi square = 3.62726 DF = 2 P = .163

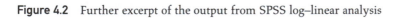

Figure 4.2 Further excerpt of the output from SPSS log–linear analysis

that there are a number of related psychological factors, such as body image, depression, anxiety and obsessive–compulsive disorder.

Lyon et al. collected data on 43 female respondents aged between 11 and 19 admitted to an Eating Disorder Program during a 14-month period. The data, including measures of biogenetic predisposition, individual characteristics and family functioning, was presented in a table.

Log–linear analysis was run on two four-way interactions. In the first four-way analysis Lyon et al. found that a family history of depression, feelings of ineffectiveness and low interoceptive awareness (interoceptive means sensitivity to pain originating outside the body) were significant for individuals diagnosed with anorexia. The significant two-way interactions were: (1) anorexia × family history of depression; (2) feelings of ineffectiveness × low interoceptive awareness; (3) anorexia × low interoceptive awareness; (4) anorexia × feelings of ineffectiveness.

The second four-way analysis included variables concerned with family history of eating disorders, childhood behaviour and within-family dependence. These variables failed to reach significance. The authors were surprised about this and cite literature which supported the idea that these variables are related to anorexia. They suggest that the fault may lie in their sample.

From health

Health and medicine frequently collect categorical data. Data like age, income, gender, treatment type and the like is standard in many clinical trials or, indeed, hospital data collection. Log–linear analysis thus lends itself to analysing this type of data and searches of medline, for instance, yield a variety of studies using log–linear analysis to look at the strength of associations between categorical variables.

Cooper et al. (2004) report some of the important associations for compliance with transdermal nicotine substitution, the so-called 'patch' to help smokers quit. Their sample was fairly large ($n = 619$) and employed a population of males and females aged 18 or older. Their most significant findings were that remaining within the study (chi-square change = 13.94 and $p < .001$) and more intensive treatment (chi-square change = 14.96 and $p = .005$) were associated with better adherence to treatment at the end of the study and at follow-up at the six-month point. Often studies such as this implicate level of income with treatment success and the authors of this study highlight the fact that they did not find any such relationship.

From business

In business, decisions are often made by consensus of a number of individuals. Tihanyi and Ellstrand (1998) examined the involvement of the board of directors and other stakeholders in decisions to enter new markets. Firms were coded '0' or '1' depending on whether they had made investments in emerging economies. Tihanyi and Ellstrand looked at a number of factors contributing to these decisions and found, through log–linear analysis, that institutional investors, prior performance and the interaction of prior performance and board structure were significant. They were then able to determine the probability, given these interactions, that investment in emerging economies would take place. One of their disproved hypotheses was that board structure on its own had a significant effect on decision to invest: it did not, but the interaction of prior performance and board structure did have a significant effect. This means that neither prior performance nor board structure on their own were significant but the interaction between the two was.

FAQs

Which are the independent and which are the dependent variables in log–linear analysis?

No distinction is made as we are looking at associations between variables and not necessarily at effects.

What is the difference between log–linear analysis and chi-square?

Although log–linear can be used with two variables it is often used with three or more. One of the limitations of chi-square is that it is limited to just two variables. Both tests are for association and start with contingency tables, but whereas chi-square allows determination of an association somewhere within the data, log–linear analysis allows a model to be developed that determines where those associations are.

What about missing data?

The problem here is with expected frequencies: if these are low then statistical power is reduced. There are a number of ways to get around this. Collapsing data and combining categories is one way, though this must be guided by sound theoretical judgement. Another way is to add some constant such as 0.5 to every cell so that all zero-value cells are eliminated.

SUMMARY

Log–linear analysis is useful when there is a contingency table with two or more categorical variables. There should be five times as many cases as there are cells in the contingency table. In log–linear analysis one tries to develop a model which keeps a fit between the expected and observed cell frequencies while removing associations or interactions between variables which do not add to the fit of the model.

GLOSSARY

Complete or total independence model   in chi-square analysis the null hypothesis is that the variables are totally independent and thus have no associations.

Frequency or contingency table   a method of organising data into rows and columns composed of cells.

Log–linear   a method of analysing two or more (often three, though) categorical variables in a contingency table with the aim of determining associations among these variables.

Saturated and unsaturated   a saturated model in log–linear analysis is one where all the variables and interactions are present. In an unsaturated one, not all of them are present.

REFERENCES

Cooper, T., DeBon, M., Stockton, M., Klesges, R., Steenbergh, T., Sherrill-Mittelman, D., Jennings, L. and Johnson, K. (2004). *Addictive Behaviour*, 29 (8), 1565–1578.
Kinnear, P. and Gray, C. (2000). *SPSS for Windows Made Simple: Release 10*. Hove: Psychology Press.
Lakhan, V. and Lavalle, P. (2002). Use of log–linear models to assess factors influencing concern for the natural environment. *Environmental Management*, 30, 77–87.
Lyon, M., Chatoor, I., Atkins, D., Silber, T., Mosimann, J. and Gray, J. (1997). Testing the hypothesis of multidimensional model of anorexia nervosa in adolescents. *Adolescence*, 32, 101–111.
Tabachnick, B. and Fiddell, L. (1996). *Using Multivariate Statistics* (3rd edn). New York: HarperCollins.
Tihanyi, L. and Ellstrand, A. (1998). The involvement of board of directors and institutional investors in investing in transitional economies: an agency theory approach. *Journal of International Management*, 4, 337–351.

FURTHER READING

Agresti, A. (2002). *Categorical Data Analysis*. Hoboken, NJ: Wiley.
Bishop, Y., Fienberg, S. and Holland, P. (1975). *Discrete Multivariate Analysis Theory and Practice*. Cambridge, MA: The MIT Press.
Everitt, B. and Dunn, G. (2001). *Applied Multivariate Data Analysis*. London: Arnold.

5

Logistic Regression

WHAT LOGISTIC REGRESSION IS

Logistic regression analysis predicts the values on one dependent variable from one or more independent (predicting) variables when the dependent variable is dichotomous (meaning that it divides the respondents or cases into two exclusive groups such as having a particular illness and not having it). Given that we have data on attributes of recruits to the police force, for example, we can predict whether they will or will not complete their initial training successfully. It can also be used, and this is its more common aim, to identify which predictor variables do predict the outcome and their comparative value in making the prediction. For example, we might find that the police officer recruits' family size does not predict their success at training, and that their school attainment is a better predictor of their success than their family income.

WHEN DO YOU NEED LOGISTIC REGRESSION?

Logistic regression is used when the measure on the predicted variable is dichotomous. (There are more complex forms which can deal with situations where the predicted variable takes more than two categories, when it is then referred to as polychotomous or multinomial logistic regression.) It is worth noting that many multi-category or even continuous variables can be reduced to dichotomous ones. If you had measured people's health condition on a seven-category scale from 'completely healthy' to 'terminal condition', you could reduce this to two categories such as 'healthy' and 'unhealthy'. If you had measured people's income you could reduce this to a dichotomous scale by forming two categories such as 'below median income' and 'at or above median income'. (There are of course many other ways you could divide the scale into just two categories.)

Table 5.1 Hypothetical data on retention of men and women recruits

	Stayed	Left
Men	150	300
Women	50	150

What kinds of questions does logistic regression answer? Suppose we have divided respondents into two groups on an outcome (dependent variable) measure, such as whether or not they have a criminal record by the age of 21. We have also collected data on these respondents on a number of other attributes, such as their school attainment, truancy history, number of siblings, economic status, introversion. (The independent variables can be categorical or continuous and do not have to be normally distributed.) The types of questions with which logistic regression is concerned include these: Question 1: do the independent variables predict which of the two categories on the dependent variable the person falls into? Question 2: are all the independent variables predicting the outcome or only some of them? Question 3: which of the independent variables are most useful for predicting the outcome?

Logistic regression is reminiscent of multiple regression, and although we have generally tried to make the chapters in this book free-standing, we do recommend that you read the first sections of the chapter on multiple regression (up to the section 'What kinds of data are needed?') if you have not already done so. As the name implies, there are some similarities between logistic regression and multiple regression, but logistic regression is the more flexible technique because it makes no assumptions about the nature of the relationship between the independent variables and the dependent variable and the predictors do not have to be normally distributed. (Although the power of the analysis is increased if the independent variables are normally distributed and do have a linear relationship with the dependent variable.)

An important feature of logistic regression is the concepts of odds and odds ratios, so we shall explain these first. Imagine we have collected data on 650 recruits to an organisation, and recorded the sex of each one and whether or not they are still working for the organisation after one year (stayed) or not (left). The data might look like that shown in Table 5.1. You can see that there were 450 men recruits and 200 women, that 150 of the men and 50 of the women had stayed.

What are the odds of a man being in the 'Stayed' group? They are found by taking the number in the stay group and expressing them as a fraction of the non-stay (left) group. Here the odds are 150/300 = 0.5. For the women, the odds of being in the stay group are found in the same way and are 50/150 = 0.33. If we divide the odds for men by the odds for women, we obtain the odds ratio.

Here it is 0.5/0.33 = 1.52. This means that the men are one and a half times more likely to stay than the women. This odds ratio is one measure of the association between the two variables (in this example, sex and leaving/staying). If there were no association between the two variables, the odds for the two sexes would be the same and the ratio would be 1. (You may have asked why the odds for men were divided by those for women, and the answer is that it does not matter. If you divided the odds for women by those for men, 0.33/0.5 = 0.66; the women are two-thirds as likely to be stayers compared with the men.) The odds ratio just calculated is concerned with a situation with just one independent variable (sex). If there is more than one independent variable, the calculation is more compli-cated; when the odds ratio is calculated taking into account other independent variables, it is referred to as the adjusted odds ratio.

Odds ratios can be tested for statistical significance, by testing them against the null hypothesis that the ratio is 1 (when there is no relationship between the depen-dent and independent variables). This is done using the Wald test (a form of chi-square) or by looking at the confidence intervals. If the 95% confidence limits for the odds ratio do not include 1, you can conclude it is significantly different from 1.

The value of odds such as the 0.5 odds for men to be in the stay group can be expressed as natural logs (the power to which e or 2.71828 must be raised to equal the number); the natural log for 0.5 is −0.6931. (The value is negative if the number is less than 1.) This log odds is known as the logit.

In logistic regression, the program (it always is a program – nobody would try this any other way) finds a regression equation which predicts the log odds of being in one of the two groups on the dependent variable:

$$\text{log odds} = a + b \text{ (predictor)}$$

It does this by choosing an equation, seeing how well it predicts the data by look-ing at the residuals (the difference between the predicted values and the actual values), adjusting the values of a and b and re-examining how well the predic-tion fits the data. It goes through this process a number of times and comes to a stop when the best linear combination of predictor variables has been found.

If there are two or more independent variables, the equation is expanded to:

$$\text{log odds} = a + b_1 \text{ (predictor}_1) + b_2 \text{(predictor}_2) + b_3 \text{(predictor}_3) \ldots$$

The calculations become more complex, but the principle is the same.

DIFFERENT TYPES OF LOGISTIC REGRESSION

There are three types of logistic regression which are most frequently used: direct, sequential and stepwise. They differ in the rules applied in deciding which independent variables should be included in the final model or regression equation.

In the direct or enter method of logistic regression all the independent variables are forced into the regression equation. This method is generally used when there are no specific hypotheses about the order or importance of the predictors. For example, on the basis of previous research it might be assumed that compliance to medication (Yes/No) would be predicted by low side effects, high responses to treatment and insight into illness. A researcher could enter these variables into a direct logistic regression to predict medication compliance. The direct method is not appropriate if the researcher is trying to test a hypothesis concerning the relative importance of the predictor variables; in this case, the sequential method should be used.

In sequential logistic regression the researcher determines the order in which the independent variables are entered into the model or equation. It allows one to determine the individual predictive value of the independent variables as well as the predictive value of the model as a whole (i.e. the complete set of predictor variables). In the sequential procedure, the independent variable entered in the model first is given priority and all subsequent variables are assessed to determine whether they significantly add to the predictive value of the first variable. (This method is not available in all computerised statistical packages, but as an alternative the direct method can be repeated. One starts by running direct logistic regression with some of the independent variables included and then runs it again with additional independent variables included, and compares the output from the two runs to see if adding the extra variables increases the effectiveness of the model. The effectiveness of one model can be compared with that of another by calculating a chi-square value: find the difference between log-likelihood values of the two models and multiply it by 2.)

The third procedure, stepwise logistic regression, is an exploratory method concerned with hypothesis generation. The inclusion or exclusion of independent variables in the regression equation is decided on statistical grounds as the model is run. In some statistical packages it is possible when using the stepwise method to set the significance level or chi-square value which will determine when the variables will be excluded from the model. It may also be possible to set the total number of independent variables to be included in the final model regardless of the number of variables initially entered. In a stepwise model, high correlations between the independent variables can mean that a variable will be 'thrown out' of the model when it does in fact significantly predict the dependent variable, because independent variables entered earlier have already accounted for the predictions. Therefore, it is important to select independent variables which are highly correlated with the dependent variable but have only low or no correlations with the other independent variables. This is a concern for all regression techniques but is of particular relevance to the stepwise method owing to the way variables to be kept in the model are selected.

The results from a logistic regression produce a number of models, or regression equations, such as the constant model (which contains only the constant), the perfect model, the full model (which contains all the predictors), the incomplete model (which contains some of the predictors). They can be compared to see which produces a better prediction. The constant model is likely to provide the worst fit for the data. The full model contains all the independent variables entered into the model as well as the constant. Generally, if this model does not improve the prediction of the dependent variable compared with the constant model, then the chosen independent variables are not related to outcome. (If any model which includes the predictor variables does not fit the data better than the constant model, which does not include any of them, then the predictor variables are not in fact predicting.) An incomplete model contains some of the independent variables and the constant. The perfect model is a hypothetical model which maximises the allocation of the participants to the correct group on the dependent variable. The perfect model can be compared with the full model or an incomplete model to determine their relative strengths; it is hoped to obtain a non-significant result, showing that the model being tested is not different from the perfect one.

The general aim in comparing these different models is to choose a model which is effective in predicting the dependent variable from those independent variables selected. The chosen model will be a regression equation of the kind described earlier:

$$\text{log odds} = a + b_1 (\text{predictor}_1) + b_2 (\text{predictor}_2) + b_3 (\text{predictor}_3) \dots$$

The overall significance of a model (including the constant and any number of predictors) can be tested using a goodness-of-fit test such as the likelihood ratio chi-square test to compare the goodness of fit of the model with that of the constant only model. If the outcome is non-significant, this indicates that there is no difference in predictive power between the model which includes none of the independent variables and the model which includes all the independent variables.

It is suggested by some researchers that rather than using goodness-of-fit statistics you should examine the proportion of cases which the analysis has managed to classify into the correct group. This proportion demonstrates the usefulness of the independent variables for identifying particular cases.

The constant and the regression coefficients or beta values (b_1, b_2, etc.) for the predictors are displayed in the output from any regression model by most computer packages. In logistic regression they are evaluated using a Wald statistic which is given for each predictor in the regression models, with its corresponding significance value. The Wald statistic is the regression coefficient divided by the corresponding standard error, a type of z statistic, and can be used to determine the significance of each of the regressors in the model.

WHAT KINDS OF DATA ARE NEEDED?

The dependent or predicted variable is dichotomous so that respondents are divided into two exclusive categories. (There are special forms of logistic regression for dealing with matched groups.) The independent or predicting variables can be continuous, categorical or nominal.

HOW MUCH DATA? (HOW MANY RESPONDENTS FOR HOW MANY INDEPENDENT VARIABLES?)

Problems arise if there are too few cases relative to the number of predictors. Tabachnik and Fiddell (1996) say this can lead to excessively high coefficients for the predictors or very large standard errors; they advise various alternatives if this happens, the simplest of which is to remove one or more predictor variables from the analysis.

WHICH INDEPENDENT VARIABLES TO INCLUDE?

The outcome of any regression procedure depends on the variables included in it. If a variable is a strong predictor of the dependent variable but is not included in the data being analysed, it cannot reveal its predictive power. So the researcher needs to select the independent variables carefully, ensuring ones which are likely to predict the dependent variable are included.

Logistic regression can include interactions between the independent variables. Interaction means that the effect of one independent variable differs according to the level of another independent variable. (For example, having a high or low level of pay may predict whether people are or are not satisfied with their jobs, but this may be true for those in 'factory-floor' jobs and not true for those in 'white-collar' jobs.)

TECHNICAL CONSIDERATIONS AND SCREENING THE DATA

It is inappropriate to enter into the same regression model independent variables which are highly correlated with each other, because they will mask each other's effects: if variable X predicts the dependent variable and variable Y also does, but variables X and Y are themselves correlated, then the predictive power of variable X will obscure the predictive power of variable Y. (This is the issue of multicollinearity described in the chapter on multiple regression.) So the correlation between independent variables should be examined and if two of them are highly correlated (say 0.7 or more) then one of them should be dropped and not included in the analysis. (Point biserial correlations can be performed between a continuous and a dichotomous variable.)

Outliers (i.e. extremely high or low scores compared with the others on an independent variable) also influence the results of the regression model. Examining the distribution of scores on an independent variable can suggest if there are any outliers. If the scores are transformed into standardised (z) scores, any where the z score is ±3.29 or more may be classed as outliers. Outliers can legitimately be excluded from the data set.

HOW DO YOU DO LOGISTIC REGRESSION?

The usual logistic regression analysis takes place in stages. First, it determines whether there is a relationship between the outcome and the predictor(s); if there is not, there is no point proceeding. Assuming there is a relationship between a set of predictors and the dependent variable, the analysis determines whether this relationship can be simplified by reducing the number of predictors without decreasing the predictive value of the model. It can also show the best set of predictors from those included, and one can use the results to predict the outcome for new participants.

There are two less common types of analysis, probit and multinomial. Probit analysis is similar to logistic regression except that it assumes a normal distribution underlies the dependent variable. It is frequently used in medical science. Multinomial regression is used when the dependent variable is categorical but not dichotomous; in other words, it has more than two categories. For example, salary may be categorised as high, medium, low. If the dependent variable has more than two categories, one alternative technique for analysing the data is discriminant analysis. In discriminant analysis the dependent variable needs to be categorical, the independent variables have to be continuous, and it is assumed that the relationship between the two is linear. The researcher attempts to determine membership of the groups of the dependent variable on the basis of one or a number of independent variables.

LIMITATIONS OF LOGISTIC REGRESSION

When considering the use of any regression technique, it is important to remember two points. First, if one variable predicts another this does not imply causality. Second, with a large sample even trivially small correlations can become significant, and it is necessary to bear in mind that statistical significance does not necessarily imply practical significance.

EXAMPLE OF LOGISTIC REGRESSION AND ITS INTERPRETATION

In order to indicate how logistic regression works, we shall explain the output obtained from SPSS for a particular analysis. The study was concerned with predicting the gender of the participants. Participants completed a task where they had to detect the presence of an auditory signal. In this task the number of errors (labelled TOT_FP in the output) and the reaction time when responding (labelled MEANTIME) were two of the variables examined. Participants also completed a questionnaire assessing the lifetime occurrence of psychiatric symptoms which yielded a score labelled PSYCHTRA. Figure 5.1 shows the first part of the output. The Enter method of regression was used, forcing all the variables into the model at once and retaining them in the model.

The first table (Case Processing Summary) in Figure 5.1 shows that data from 54 participants (from a total sample of 106) is complete and included in the analysis. The next table (Dependent Variable Encoding) displays the coding used for the dependent variable: a value of 0 is shown to mean 'male' and a value of 1 is shown to mean 'female'.

The information displayed next is concerned with the constant model. This initial stage of the analysis is referred to as Step or Block 0. The Classification Table is like a cross-tabulation of the dependent variable's predicted values. Here being female has the positive value so the analysis is concerned with the correct classification of all female participants as being female on the basis of their scores on the independent variables. This may sound a little strange but it is merely an extension of the linear regression model, except that rather than predicting high or low scores on a variable it is concerned with being in one group or another. The table headed Variables in the Equation displays what is included in the analysis, in this case the constant only. It gives the beta values (B), the beta value standard error (S.E.), the Wald statistic, its degrees of freedom (df) and related significance values for the model. The Exp(B) column is the estimated odds ratio for the constant: it is the value of B exponentiated, which means it is the value of e to the power of B or in this case $e^{.074}$. The Variables not in the Equation table gives the statistics Score, degrees of freedom (df) and significance values (Sig.) for the variables not included in the model. The Score value is the result from a test to determine whether the coefficient is significantly different from zero in terms of the log-likelihood of predicting the dependent variable.

The remainder of the output from the analysis is shown in Figure 5.2. The Enter method of regression means there is only one step in the analysis which includes all the variables entered into the model. The Omnibus Tests of Model Coefficients table considers the goodness of fit of the model in this step, block and model. Since all the variables were placed in one block and the Enter regression method were used, the chi-square values are all the same. It can be seen that the

Logistic Regression

Case Processing Summary

Unweighted Cases[a]		N	Percent
Selected Cases	Included in Analysis	54	50.9
	Missing Cases	52	49.1
	Total	106	100.0
Unselected Cases		0	.0
Total		106	100.0

a. If weight is in effect, see classification table for the total number of cases.

Dependent Variable Encoding

Original Value	Internal Value
male	0
female	1

Block 0: Beginning Block

Classification Table[a, b]

			Predicted		
			SEX		Percentage
Observed			male	female	Correct
Step 0	SEX	male	0	26	.0
		female	0	28	100.0
	Overall Percentage				51.9

a. Constant is included in the model.
b. The cut value is .500.

Variables in the Equation

		B	S.E.	Wald	df	Sig.	Exp(B)
Step 0	Constant	.074	.272	.074	1	.786	1.077

Variables not in the Equation

			Score	df	Sig.
Step 0	Variables	TOT_FP	4.872	1	.027
		MEANTIME	3.799	1	.051
		PSYCHTRA	3.594	1	.058
	Overall Statistics		16.400	3	.001

Figure 5.1 Example of SPSS output from logistic regression

Block 1: Method = Enter

Omnibus Tests of Model Coefficients

		Chi-square	df	Sig.
Step 1	Step	18.952	3	.000
	Block	18.952	3	.000
	Model	18.952	3	.000

Model Summary

Step	−2 Log likelihood	Cox & Snell R Square	Nagelkerke R Square
1	55.834	.296	.395

Classification Table[a]

			Predicted		
			SEX		Percentage Correct
Observed			male	female	
Step 1	SEX	male	17	9	65.4
		female	8	20	71.4
	Overall Percentage				68.5

a. The cut value is .500.

Variables in the Equation

		B	S.E.	Wald	df	Sig.	Exp(B)
Step 1[a]	TOT_FP	0.92	0.36	6.612	1	.010	1.096
	MEANTIME	−16.382	6.814	5.780	1	.016	.000
	PSYCHTRA	−13.511	5.115	6.976	1	.008	.000
	Constant	15.722	5.706	7.593	1	.006	6729465

a. Variable(s) entered on step 1: TOT_FP, MEANTIME, PSYCHTRA.

Figure 5.2 Example of further SPSS output from logistic regression

chi-square value is significant ($p < 0.01$), indicating that the variables included, when combined, are significant predictors of the gender of the participants.

The Model Summary table displays three goodness-of-fit measures: McFadden's −2 log-likelihood statistic (a very conservative measure), Cox and Snell's R^2 (which accounts for sample size and is based on log-likelihoods), and

Nagelkerke's R^2 (an adjusted form of Cox and Snell's R^2). To the non-expert, any of these measures is as good as the others, but one should select which one to use and keep to it. The R^2 values are the most readily understood since if multiplied by 100 they indicate the percentage of variance accounted for by the models.

The Classification Table in Figure 5.2 shows the number of participants correctly classified on the dependent variable. (This table can be compared directly with the one produced by the constant model and included in Figure 5.1.) It seems that some individuals cannot be correctly classified on the basis of the covariates entered since the overall percentage is not 100. In the table Variables in the Equation, all the variables are listed with their relevant statistics. The significance column shows that all of the variables reach the significance threshold of $p < 0.05$. From this analysis it would be concluded that all of the independent variables included in the model predict the gender of the participants.

EXAMPLES OF THE USE OF LOGISTIC REGRESSION

From psychology

Goodwin and Gotlib (2004) were concerned with the difference between the sexes in rate of depression, and examined whether the personality dimension of neuroticism was an influence on it. Their respondent sample consisted of 3032 individuals in the USA. To assess depression, Goodwin and Gotlib used a measure called the Composite International Diagnostic Interview Short Form (CIDI-SF); personality traits were measured using the Midlife Development Inventory (MIDI). They summarise the logistic regression part of their data analysis: 'multiple logistic regression analyses were conducted to determine the association between gender and depression, adjusting for differences in age, marital status, race and education. Analyses were then additionally adjusted for neuroticism in the relationship between gender and major depression' (p. 137). They ran three separate regression models, with 'having major depression in the last 12 months' as the dependent variable. In model 1, only gender was entered as a predictor variable. In the second model, age, marital status, race and education were also entered. In the third model, neuroticism was added.

Goodwin and Gotlib present the odds ratio (and the associated confidence intervals) for each predictor, highlighting the odds ratios which differ from 1 at the 5% significance level. In their third model the odds ratio for gender was 1.34 and for neuroticism was 2.91. They conclude 'the third model ... showed that although being female remained significantly associated with increased likelihood of major depression, neuroticism contributed significantly to the relationship between gender and depression' (p. 139).

From health

Chan and Huak (2004) surveyed a group of doctors and nurses and used multiple logistic regression to investigate the predictors of emotional health, which was divided into two categories. One category included those who scored 5 or more on the General Health Questionnaire, a 28-item test aimed at detecting psychiatric disorder, and the other included those who scored less than 5. For nurses, the predictors named as 'having posttraumatic stress disorder' (odds ratio 17.2), 'work pressure' (odds ratio 1.2) and '(work environment) innovation' (odds ratio 0.81) were all significantly predictive of emotional health. (The odds ratio value of less than 1 for innovation meant that 'those who reported that there was less emphasis on variety, change and new approaches tend to have poorer emotional health' (p. 211)).

FAQs

What do interactions in the predictors actually mean? What would an example of one in a real-world setting be?

An interaction in the predictors demonstrates that the two variables have a multiple effect: that is, having one variable is not necessarily highly predictive of outcome but when this variable co-exists in the presence of another, the second variable 'intensifies' the predictive value of the variables. In the mental health literature there are many examples of gene–environment interactions which are real-world instances of the interactions described. For example, depressive episodes (Yes/No) may be predicted by maladaptive coping strategies and number of life events. On their own, maladaptive coping strategies and life events may only be moderate predictors of depression episodes but when both variables co-exist (interact) they become strong predictors of depressive episodes.

What do I do when the variable I want to predict has more than two categories?

The logistic regression model can be extended to incorporate multiple levels of categorical variable. It is then known as a discrete choice, multinomial, polychotomous or polytomous logistic regression model.

SUMMARY

Logistic regression analysis predicts the values on one dichotomous dependent variable from one or more independent variables and can be used to compare predictors' value in making the prediction. It finds a regression equation which predicts the log odds of being in one of the two groups on the dependent variable. In the direct or enter method all the independent variables are forced into the regression equation. In sequential logistic regression the researcher determines the order in which the independent variables are entered into the model. In stepwise logistic regression, independent variables are included or excluded from the regression equation depending on statistical criteria.

The results produce a number of models, or regression equations. An incomplete model contains some of the independent variables and the constant and the aim is to obtain a model which is effective in predicting the dependent variable.

GLOSSARY

Maximum likelihood method   the method used to decide the line of best fit in logistic regression. It seeks to maximise the number of observed values which fit the regression coefficient produced by the regression model.

Predicted   the dependent variables in regression.

Predictors   the independent variables in regression.

REFERENCES

Chan, A.O.M. and Huak, C.Y. (2004). Influence of work on emotional health in health care setting. *Occupational Medicine*, 54, 207–212.

Goodwin, R.D. and Gotlib, I.H. (2004). Gender differences in depression: the role of personality factors. *Psychiatry Research*, 126, 135–142.

Tabachnick, B.G. and Fidell, L.S. (1996). *Using Multivariate Statistics* (3rd edn). New York: HarperCollins.

FURTHER READING

Harrell, F. (2001). *Regression Modeling Strategies: with applications to linear models, logistic regression, and survival analysis*. New York: Springer.

Hosmer, D.W. and Lemeshow, S. (1989). *Applied Logistic Regression*. New York: Wiley.

Jaccard, J. (2001). *Interaction Effects in Logistic Regression*. New York: Sage.

Menard, S. (2001). *Applied Logistic Regression Analysis*. New York: Sage.

Pampel, F.C. (2000). *Logistic Regression: A Primer*. Thousand Oaks, CA: Sage.

INTERNET SOURCE

www.ex.ac.uk/~SEGLea/multvar2/disclogi.htm

6

Factor Analysis

WHAT FACTOR ANALYSIS IS

Factor analysis is a technique, or more accurately, sets of techniques for identifying the underlying hypothetical constructs to account for the relationship between variables. Principal components analysis is extremely similar, and is often used as a preliminary stage to factor analysis itself. Exploratory factor analysis is used to identify the hypothetical constructs in a set of data, while confirmatory factor analysis, as the name implies, is used to confirm the existence of these hypothetical constructs in a fresh set of data. Confirmatory factor analysis is less common and has strong similarities to structural equation modelling.

WHEN DO YOU NEED FACTOR ANALYSIS?

A major issue concerns the structure of psychological constructs such as intelligence, personality, job or patient satisfaction. You might start with a large number of questions which you think measure the construct and obtain responses to these questions from a number of respondents. The responses are then correlated with each other, and factor analysis is used to see whether the items suggest there is one underlying construct or more than one. Is intelligence a single dimension or are there a number of different kinds such as social intelligence, musical intelligence, etc.? You might assess individuals' performance on a task by rating each person on a number of different attributes such as speed, neatness, elegance, skilfulness. Are the attributes really different or are the correlations between the ratings such that you are in fact using just one or two dimensions?

The study of attitudes is important in many fields, and the measurement of attitudes using attitude scales is frequently needed. This is often accomplished by presenting respondents with a number of statements and inviting them to indicate the extent of their agreement or disagreement with each one. It then becomes

	V1	V2	V3	V4	V5	V6
V1	1.000	.800	.807	.128	.283	.186
V2	.800	1.000	.936	.080	.212	.172
V3	.807	.936	1.000	.106	.282	.220
V4	.128	.080	.106	1.000	.550	.641
V5	.283	.212	.282	.550	1.000	.610
V6	.186	.172	.220	.641	.610	1.000

Figure 6.1   A correlation matrix

important to know whether one is measuring one single attitude or whether a number of attitudes are involved.

So the types of questions for which factor analysis is relevant include: (1) are the various items in this questionnaire measuring one construct? (For example, if you have a questionnaire which claims to measure patient satisfaction, are all the questions measuring a single dimension or are there two or more separate dimensions?) (2) Can a large number of variables be reduced to a smaller number? (For example, if you measure patient satisfaction by asking a set of questions about waiting time, clarity of diagnosis, consultation length, etc., can you reduce the set of measures to scores on a smaller number of underlying factors?)

PRINCIPAL COMPONENTS ANALYSIS AND FACTOR ANALYSIS

The easiest way of explaining how principal components analysis and factor analysis operate is to use an example, so suppose you have given a group of 100 people seven questions or tests, and correlated the results for each pair of variables. If you tabulated the correlations, you would obtain a table like that shown in Figure 6.1 which is known as a correlation matrix and shows the correlation between each variable and every other variable. (The table is redundant, in that the lower half below the diagonal which runs from top left to bottom right is a mirror image of the upper half.) In Figure 6.1, the correlation between V1 and V2 is .800 while the correlation between V2 and V3 is .936. You will see that variables V1, V2 and V3 correlate together quite highly and none of these correlate very much with V4, V5 and V6; on the other hand V4, V5 and V6 do correlate with each other quite highly (.55 to .64). So this suggests there are two underlying factors, one explaining the correlations between variables V1, V2, V3 and another separate one explaining the correlations between V4, V5 and V6.

Principal components analysis (PCA) and factor analysis are both procedures for analysing the correlation matrix to find the underlying constructs or latent variables which explain the pattern of correlations it contains and how far each one is measured by each of the variables. In PCA, a set of correlated variables is transformed into a set of uncorrelated variables, the components, which are expected to be smaller than the set of the original variables. Factor analysis (FA) is similar, but yields factors rather than components (although it is usual to refer to the outcome of both PCA and FA as factors). With both procedures, a large set of measures is reduced to a smaller set of factors which explain the maximum amount of variance in the bivariate correlations.

In a correlation matrix such as that shown in Figure 6.1, the entries in the diagonal running from top left to bottom right are the correlations of each test with itself and are referred to as communalities. These will be 1.00 if you calculate the correlation between each test and itself from the data you have obtained from your respondents.

The distinction between PCA and FA is that in PCA the communalities are left as 1.00, so all the variance in the variables is being analysed. But in FA the communalities are replaced by estimates rather than the actual values of 1.0. Why should you use estimates when you have the actual values? To simplify matters very much, by using estimated communalities you are analysing only the variance shared by the scores of the respondents on the variables; error and specific variance (variance arising just from the particular variable) are removed. If communalities of 1 are used, error and specific variance are included. In practice, the outcome of the two procedures is often quite similar. (It has been suggested that whether one puts 1 or an estimate of communality in the diagonal will have little effect on the outcome so long as there are 30 variables and the communalities are over 0.4.)

Both PCA and FA produce a set of components (in PCA) or factors (in FA) with the first one accounting for the largest amount of variance in the sets of scores, the second accounting for the next largest amount not already explained by the first factor, the third accounting for the next largest amount not already explained by the previous ones, and so on. In PCA the factors are not correlated with each other, and this is also true in FA unless one requests oblique rotation (which is explained later).

WHAT KINDS OF DATA ARE NEEDED?

To perform factor analysis the data should meet certain requirements. The fundamental ones are (1) data has been measured on an interval scale (although it can be used with dichotomous data); (2) respondents vary in their scores on the variables; (3) the scores on the variables have linear correlations with each other; (4) the scores on the variables are normally distributed.

1 Data has been measured on an interval scale: Many measures of attitude use a Likert type of response in which the respondents indicate whether they agree or disagree with a statement using a five- or seven-point scale. It has become common to assume that Likert scales are interval.

Despite what has just been said, it is possible to apply FA to dichotomous variables such as yes/no responses; Kline (1994, p. 126), discussing test construction, recommends the use of the phi-coefficient as the measure of correlation in such cases.

2 Respondents vary in their scores on the variables: If there is no variation in the scores between the respondents, it is impossible to calculate a correlation coefficient. Since correlations are the basis on which FA builds, variation in the scores is essential.

3 The scores on the variables have linear correlations with each other: FA works on the correlations between items, and if the items do not correlate then it is not sensible to do it. One can look at scatterplots of the relationship between pairs of variables to see if the relationship looks linear, and certainly should examine the original correlation matrix to see if there are items which do not correlate with any others. You would expect most of the correlations in the correlation matrix to be 0.30 or more. If there are variables with very low correlations with all the others, it is sensible to leave them out of the FA since they cannot contribute to a factor. Conversely, if two items correlate very highly (0.90 or more) then they are redundant and you would drop one of them from the analysis. If they are both left in, they may yield a factor of their own, which is known as a 'bloated specific'.

4 The scores on the variables should be normally distributed: This is not quite true: Tabachnick and Fidell (1996) point out that if you are using PCA or FA descriptively there is no need to make assumptions about the shape of the distribution. But if statistical inference is used to determine the number of factors, normal distributions are assumed. One can look at the distribution of scores on each of the variables. If any are highly skewed, a transformation can be applied to make them normally distributed, which means the square root or log of the scores is substituted for the original ones. (Doing this makes understanding more difficult, and it is not recommended for the non-expert.)

HOW MUCH DATA? (HOW MANY RESPONDENTS FOR HOW MANY INDEPENDENT VARIABLES?)

There is no firm rule to say how many respondents must have provided data before FA is firmly based. Essentially, the more respondents' data you have, the better, but this is not very helpful if you want to know the minimum number. Tabachnick and Fidell (1996) describe a situation where one has 300 respondents as 'comforting', but Kline (1994) believes samples of 100 are sufficient so long as there are at least twice as many respondents as variables. This ratio is lower than many recommend. Child (1990) argues that the number of respondents required depends on the average correlation between the variables being analysed; if it is 0.5, he suggests about one and a half times as many respondents as variables, whereas if it is 0.1 six times as many respondents as variables are needed. Bryman and Cramer (1997) follow other authorities in recommending at least 100 respondents and at least five times as many respondents as variables, so with 100 respondents one should have no more than 20 variables.

Kline (1994) discusses the value of having heterogeneous respondents, meaning respondents who do not obtain similar scores on the variables being measured. If all the respondents had a similar score on one variable, the correlation of that variable with any other will be low and this will distort the outcome of the FA. It is sensible to look at the distribution of scores on each variable, and delete from the analysis any which show little variation across respondents.

HOW MANY VARIABLES TO INCLUDE?

Kline (1994) suggests there should be at least three variables for each factor, while Tabachnick and Fidell (1996) recommend five or six variables per factor. The basic idea is to have a number of variables for each factor so that there are correlations in which it can be revealed. If you had just one variable measuring a factor, it would not correlate with any other variables and would not feature in the results of an FA which is essentially an analysis of correlations. So if you are devising a measure of a construct such as patient satisfaction, include five items for each of the dimensions (such as satisfaction with the treatment, satisfaction with the consultation, satisfaction with the timeliness of consultation, etc.) which you expect to make up that overall construct.

WHICH VARIABLES TO INCLUDE?

The answer to this question depends on the aim of your research. If you are trying to establish a test of a particular construct such as patient satisfaction, you need to include a set of items which cover all aspects of patient satisfaction so far as you can judge what these are. If you are hoping to show that patient satisfaction is distinct from people's overall happiness then you would need to include variables measuring both of these constructs.

TECHNICAL CONSIDERATIONS AND SCREENING THE DATA

Once you have obtained measures on all the variables from your sample of respondents, the correlation matrix can be created and examined to see if the data meets technical requirements for FA. You can look at the matrix to confirm that most of the correlations are at least 0.3, and there are various tests which can be applied. For example, the Kaiser–Meyer–Olkin measure assesses sampling adequacy of the items. (It is the ratio of the sum of squared correlations to the sum of squared correlations plus sum of squared partial correlations. It approaches 1 if partial correlations are small.) It can vary from 0 to 1 and should be 0.6 or above; if it is less than 0.6, you can remove some of the variables and check again. Bartlett's sphericity test is used to test the null hypothesis that the variables in the population (as opposed to the sample which provided the data) are uncorrelated. If it fails to reject the null hypothesis, then strictly speaking you should not do FA as the variables are uncorrelated; but Tabachnick and Fidell suggest that the test is oversensitive and should only be used if there are fewer than five cases per variable.

HOW YOU DO FA

Exploratory FA is by far the most common form and that is what is described here. It involves a sequence of steps. Not all of these are compulsory, but a typical sequence is as follows:

1 Gather data from a large number of respondents (at least 100) on a number of variables. (These might be individual questions on a test or scale.)
2 Correlate the scores on all the variables with the scores on all the others to produce a correlation matrix.
3 Examine the correlation matrix and decide whether to omit any variables from the FA because they do not correlate with any other variables.
4 Perform a PCA.
5 Examine the results of the PCA to decide how many factors there are which are worth keeping.
6 Carry out FA so that the analysis is forced to use the number of factors determined at step 5.
7 Examine the results of the FA to see how clear the outcome is.
8 Carry out the FA again, with orthogonal rotation of the factors to produce a clearer outcome.
9 Examine the results of the second FA and decide whether the outcome is clear.
10 Carry out the FA again, with oblique rotation of the factors to produce a clearer outcome.

11 Compare the results of the orthogonal and oblique FAs and decide which has simpler structure.
12 From the results of the analysis with simpler structure, interpret the factors.

This may look rather daunting, but the mathematical procedures are of course carried out by the computer in a few seconds. The collection and preparation of the data and the interpretation of the output are where the researcher spends most time!

Assume you have completed the first three steps of gathering data from a large number of respondents (at least 100) on a number of variables, correlated the scores between all the variables to produce a correlation matrix, examined the correlation matrix and deleted any variables which do not correlate with any other variables. You then start the serious analyses by proceeding to step 4 and carrying out a PCA. This will produce an initial output such as is shown in Figure 6.2, which was obtained using SPSS.

At step 5, you examine the results of the PCA (Figure 6.2) to decide how many factors to retain. In the output from the PCA, the variables are listed down the left-hand side and the initial communality of each is shown as 1.00. The next part of the output shows a list of the components and the eigenvalue and percentage of variance explained by each one. (The eigenvalue is the sum of the squared loadings of the component. The percentage of variance explained is the eigenvalue divided by the sum of the eigenvalues with the result multiplied by 100.) Those components which have an eigenvalue greater than 1 are listed separately, with the amount of variance they explain.

It is built into the PCA procedure that it will show the same number of components as there are variables in the original data set, and that the first component will account for a large percentage of variance. The components or factors are listed in order of the amount of variance explained, so after the fifth or sixth the percentages of variance typically become quite small. Studying the outcome of the PCA helps you answer the next question: how many factors should be extracted?

There are two main ways of deciding on the number of factors to extract. One is to use the eigenvalues shown in the results of the PCA. It has been a convention to retain in the analysis the number of factors shown by the PCA to have eigenvalues greater than 1 (known as Kaiser's criterion). The other is to examine a scree plot, such as that shown in Figure 6.3. In a scree plot, the eigenvalue is plotted against the component number. It is interpreted by looking for the point at which there is an 'elbow' in the line, and the number of components above this point is taken as the number of factors to be extracted from the data.

Authorities disagree over the acceptability of Kaiser's criterion. Although it is often used, Kline (1994) believes that accepting factors with an eigenvalue over 1 gives too many factors and one should use the scree test instead.

Communalities

	Initial	Extraction
V1	1.000	.834
V2	1.000	.928
V3	1.000	.934
V4	1.000	.747
V5	1.000	.703
V6	1.000	.773

Extraction Method: Principal Component Analysis.

Total Variance Explained

Component	Initial Eigenvalues			Extraction Sums of Squared Loadings		
	Total	% of Variance	Cumulative %	Total	% of Variance	Cumulative %
1	3.067	51.112	51.112	3.067	51.112	51.112
2	1.852	30.864	81.976	1.852	30.864	81.976
3	.438	7.298	89.275			
4	.352	5.871	95.145			
5	.231	3.848	98.993			
6	.060	1.007	100.000			

Extraction Method: Principal Component Analysis.

Component Matrix(a)

	Component	
	1	2
V1	.830	−.380
V2	.844	−.464
V3	.873	−.415
V4	.465	.728
V5	.609	.576
V6	.562	.677

Extraction Method: Principal Component Analysis.

a 2 components extracted.

Figure 6.2 Example of PCA results

Step 6 involves carrying out FA in such a way that the analysis is forced to use the number of factors decided upon at the previous step. There are alternative methods of FA, but it is common to perform the FA (with the specified number of factors) using the principal axis factoring method. The result will be similar to

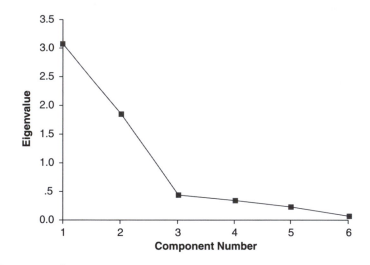

Figure 6.3   A scree plot

that shown in Figure 6.4. A factor matrix is obtained which shows the correlation of each variable with each of the factors. Another table shows the communalities for each variable, indicating the proportion of the variance for each variable explained by the solution. Another table shows the percentage of variance explained by each factor.

Step 7 involves examining the results of the FA to see how clear the outcome is and deciding whether to repeat the analysis but adding rotation of the factors. The aim of rotating the factors is to achieve simple structure, a situation in which items load highly on one factor and low on others so that interpreting what each factor is becomes simpler. In Figure 6.4 the factor matrix is not very clear because, among other things, V5 correlates .504 on factor 1 and .540 on factor 2, so one cannot really assign it to either factor. You may well therefore decide to proceed to an analysis in which the factors are rotated.

If one does decide to rotate the factors, there is still the need to decide which method of rotation to use. There are two major types: orthogonal and oblique. In orthogonal rotation, the factors remain uncorrelated with each other whereas in oblique rotation they are allowed to correlate. Under each type there are different methods which can be used. For orthogonal rotation, the most commonly used procedure is varimax, which maximises the variance between the factors so that each factor tends to load high on a small number of variables and low on the others. This makes it easier to interpret the factor. For oblique rotation, the oblimin procedure is the most frequently used alternative. It is perfectly proper to do orthogonal rotation and then oblique rotation to see which yields the clearer picture.

Factor Analysis

Factor Matrix(a)

	Factor	
	1	2
V1	.793	−.258
V2	.881	−.388
V3	.913	−.336
V4	.376	.672
V5	.504	.540
V6	.482	.679

Extraction Method: Principal Axis Factoring.

a 2 factors extracted. 10 iterations required.

Communalities

	Extraction
V1	.695
V2	.927
V3	.946
V4	.593
V5	.546
V6	.694

Extraction Method: Principal Axis Factoring.

Total Variance Explained

Factor	Extraction Sums of Squared Loadings		
	Total	% of Variance	Cumulative %
1	2.866	47.771	47.771
2	1.535	25.582	73.353

Extraction Method: Principal Axis Factoring.

Figure 6.4 Output from FA

If rotation is chosen, step 8 involves carrying out the FA again with orthogonal rotation of the factors. Figure 6.5 is an example of the output produced when the analysis was run again with orthogonal (varimax) rotation. At step 9, you examine the results of the second FA and decide whether the outcome is clear. The rotated factor matrix in Figure 6.5 is clearer than the factor matrix in Figure 6.4, with V1, V2 and V3 loading high on factor 1 and V4, V5 and V6 loading high on

Factor Analysis

Factor Matrix(a)

a 2 factors extracted. 10 iterations required.

Rotated Factor Matrix(a)

	Factor	
	1	2
V1	.821	.146
V2	.960	.072
V3	.964	.133
V4	.016	.770
V5	.191	.714
V6	.106	.826

Extraction Method: Principal Axis Factoring. Rotation Method: Varimax with Kaiser Normalisation.
a Rotation converged in 3 iterations.

Total Variance Explained

Factor	Rotation Sums of Squared Loadings		
	Total	% of Variance	Cumulative %
1	2.571	42.856	42.856
2	1.830	30.497	73.353

Extraction Method: Principal Axis Factoring.

Factor Transformation Matrix

Factor	1	2
1	.882	.471
2	−.471	.882

Extraction Method: Principal Axis Factoring. Rotation Method: Varimax with Kaiser Normalisation.

Figure 6.5   Output from FA following orthogonal (varimax) rotation

factor 2. In all cases the variable has a low loading on the other factor; the position of V5 is much clearer than it was in Figure 6.4 after the initial analysis, as it loads much higher on factor 2 than factor 1.

Step 10 is carrying out the FA again but with oblique rotation of the factors to produce a clearer outcome. If oblique rotation is used, the output is more complicated as shown in Figure 6.6. Following oblique rotation you get a factor

Factor Analysis

Factor Matrix(a)

a 2 factors extracted. 10 iterations required.

Pattern Matrix(a)

	Factor	
	1	2
V1	.822	.043
V2	.974	−.050
V3	.970	.011
V4	−.083	.787
V5	.103	.707
V6	.002	.833

Extraction Method: Principal Axis Factoring. Rotation Method: Oblimin with Kaiser Normalisation.
a Rotation converged in 3 iterations.

Total Variance Explained

Factor	Rotation Sums of Squared Loadings(a)
	Total
1	2.697
2	1.979

Extraction Method: Principal Axis Factoring.
a When factors are correlated, sums of squared loadings cannot be added to obtain a total variance.

Structure Matrix

	Factor	
	1	2
V1	.833	.247
V2	.961	.192
V3	.973	.252
V4	.112	.766
V5	.279	.732
V6	.209	.833

Extraction Method: Principal Axis Factoring. Rotation Method: Oblimin with Kaiser Normalisation.

(Continued)

Factor Correlation Matrix

Factor	1	2
1	1.000	.248
2	.248	1.000

Extraction Method: Principal Axis Factoring. Rotation Method: Oblimin with Kaiser Normalisation.

Figure 6.6 Output from FA following oblique (oblimin) rotation

structure matrix and a factor pattern matrix. These look similar, and their meanings are readily confused. Giles (2002, p. 129) states: 'after oblique rotation, the structure matrix is the table that you should use for interpretation' which contradicts Tabachnick and Fidell (2001, p. 585) who say 'Following oblique rotation, the meaning of factors is ascertained from the pattern matrix' (although they do acknowledge later that 'there is some debate as to whether one should interpret the pattern matrix or the structure matrix following oblique rotation' (p. 602)). Kline (1994, p. 63) is definite: 'The factor structure consists of the correlations of the original variables with the rotated factors ... it is important ... that the structure and not the pattern is interpreted.'

Following oblique rotation, the correlation between the two factors is shown; in Figure 6.6 it is .248.

You then compare, in step 11, the results of the orthogonal and oblique FAs and decide which has simpler structure. In our example, the structure matrix following oblique rotation in Figure 6.6 is rather less clear than the rotated factor matrix following orthogonal rotation shown in Figure 6.5, because the orthogonal rotation shows each variable loads less than .2 on the factor which is not the main one on which that variable loads. Following oblique rotation, the loadings on the 'other' factor are over .2 in four of six cases. Consequently in this instance you would probably use the outcome of the orthogonal rotation.

Finally, at step 12 you take the results of the analysis with simpler structure and interpret the factors. This means putting a name to them which reflects what they are measuring. Deciding what a factor is measuring, what it should be named, is a subjective process. You look at the items which have high loadings on the factor and devise a name which summarises them. A loading is the correlation between the item and the factor, but what is a high loading? One convention has been to use items which have a loading of 0.3 or more, although some authors have questioned the value of this policy. Certainly one should consider the practical significance of the outcome: a correlation of 0.3 means the variable is explaining 9% of the variance, and even a loading of 0.4 explains only 16%.

The data analysed in the example used in this chapter has yielded two factors. You cannot interpret them until you know what the variables were. The study which yielded the data was an investigation of people's satisfaction with a number of areas of life, and the six items were:

1 How satisfied are you with your relationship with your spouse?
2 How satisfied are you with your relationship with your children?
3 How satisfied are you with your relationship with your parents?
4 How satisfied are you with your relationship with your boss at work?
5 How satisfied are you with your relationship with your colleagues at work?
6 How satisfied are you with your relationship with your management at work?

Since items 1–3 load on factor 1 and items 4–6 on factor 2, you might think it reasonable to label factor 1 'satisfaction with family members' and factor 2 'satisfaction with people at work'. But the naming process is subjective, and you might prefer other words; they should of course reflect the content of the appropriate items.

There is a further point to make about the results of FA and it concerns cross-validation. Kline (1994, p. 181) observes that interpreting the meaning of a factor from the items loading on it is only a form of face validity. He writes: 'the failure to identify a factor other than by its loadings is about the most common form of misleading factor analytic research'. He emphasises the need to validate any factors against external criteria. So we would need some external evidence that respondents who scored highly on factor 1 in our example did have higher satisfaction with their family relationships. In addition, one would like to see the any factor solution replicated using different respondents so one could be confident it was not specific to the original respondents.

CONFIRMATORY FACTOR ANALYSIS

Confirmatory factor analysis is described by Tabachnick and Fidell as a much more sophisticated technique than exploratory factor analysis, since it is used to test a theory about latent processes (such as the existence of specified factors). In confirmatory factor analysis one attempts to demonstrate that a hypothesised factor structure fits a fresh set of data and to do so one uses structural equation modelling. In very simple terms, one constructs a model which incorporates the hypothesised factor structure and compares the data against that model to see if it fits. How well the data fits the model can be assessed by a goodness-of-fit test (of which there are different types). Kline (1994, p. 96) points out that goodness-of-fit tests yield a chi-square value, and if that is not significant this means the null hypothesis cannot be rejected – and this in turn means that the model cannot be rejected. In other words, the model does fit the data. But this does not mean that only that model fits the data – there may be others which also fit it or fit it better.

Since confirmatory factor analysis is much less common than exploratory factor analysis and is closely related to structural equation modelling, you are recommended to acquire a basic appreciation of the latter if you are planning a study involving confirmatory analysis.

EXAMPLES OF FA

From psychology

Harris (2003) used FA to study the moral emotions (shame, guilt, embarrassment), an area in which it had not previously been applied, by asking 720 Australian drivers who had been apprehended for driving while having more than the legally permitted level of alcohol in their blood to complete a 23-item questionnaire. This required respondents to answer on a five-point scale (from 'not at all' to 'felt overwhelmed by it') items asking about whether they felt ashamed, guilty or embarrassed.

A PCA of the responses to 22 items indicated that three factors explained 55% of the variance. Factors were extracted on the basis of eigenvalues greater than 1, the scree test and simple structure of the solution. The factors were rotated using oblimin. The first factor had strong loadings for items expected to measure shame and guilt, and the notion that these emotions load on one factor was seen as contrary to what the previous literature would have suggested. The second factor was labelled 'unresolved shame' as the items dealt with ongoing negative feelings. The third factor loaded on items concerning discomfort from being the centre of unwanted social attention and was labelled embarrassment–disclosure.

Harris observes that shame and guilt were not distinguishable in participants' memories of attending a criminal justice case: 'Characteristics seen as theoretically important in comparisons of the emotions were measured by the same factor … . The analyses did, however, distinguish two other shame-related emotions, embarrassment and unresolved shame, that had quite different characteristics from shame-guilt' (pp. 467–468). At a more general level, he concludes that 'The finding that shame and guilt were not distinguished between is in contrast to theoretical and empirical models that emphasize their distinctiveness' (p. 470).

From health

Measuring patient satisfaction with general practitioner services

Following pressure from the UK government for assessment of the satisfaction of patients with the services provided by general practitioners, Grogan et al. (1995)

developed a scale to measure the patients' satisfaction with particular aspects of the service they received. Grogan et al. proposed, from studying previous literature and the outcome of an initial questionnaire and interview study, that there were 10 dimensions involved in patient satisfaction: doctor information getting, doctor information giving, doctor social skills, doctor competence, doctor time pressure, access, facilities, nurses, receptionists, general satisfaction. A total of 148 items, intended to cover all 10 dimensions, were written in Likert-scale format so that there was a statement, and the respondents were asked to indicate how far they agreed or disagreed with it on a five-point scale. A sample of 1193 patients completed the questionnaire, and items which yielded heavily skewed responses were removed, as were six items intended to assess general satisfaction. The remaining items were subjected to PCA. Five factors were revealed, and items which loaded 0.5 or more on a factor were retained for the final subscales which were labelled 'doctors', 'access', 'nurses', 'appointments', 'facilities'. The first factor, 'doctors', explained over 39% of the variance in satisfaction scores. The 20 items on this subscale were analysed separately using PCA and this indicated that there was one factor underlying these items. All the five subscales had high internal reliability (Cronbach's alpha varied from 0.73 to 0.95) and correlated at over 0.45 with the general measure of satisfaction.

Some years later, Grogan et al. (2000) reported a confirmatory factor analysis of the patient satisfaction scale using 1151 completed questionnaires. The five-factor solution of the original work provided a better fit to the data than either a no-factor or a one-factor solution: 'the five-factor structure of the scale … was also confirmed' (p. 213).

The 'doctor' subscale again came out as a unitary construct 'which suggests … that patients do not differentiate between different aspects of the consultation (such as information giving, information getting, clinical competence) in terms of satisfaction' (p. 213).

From business/management

Silvester et al. (2003) set out to compare two attributional models of sales performance in terms of their effectiveness at predicting performance among retail sales assistants. As part of the study, they developed a job-specific questionnaire requiring sales assistants to judge the most likely causes of successful and unsuccessful customer interactions. A set of 80 items was devised in which respondents indicated on a five-point scale whether an outcome, such as a customer demanding to speak to the manager, was due to an internal–controllable (IC) cause ('you did not apologize immediately') or an external–uncontrollable (EU) cause ('sometimes customers can get very angry'). 'Item selection was devised to produce a set of items that were normally distributed. All items were examined for skew and kurtosis, and any item greater than ± 2 was discarded in order to minimize error variance' (p. 121). The items remaining were factor analysed using PCA and rotated to simple structure using varimax rotation.

Responses from 453 participants were collected, and the use and outcome of the FA is described as follows:

> Item selection produced a set of 33 items that were normally distributed. Pre-analysis checks were conducted including the Kaiser-Meyer-Olkin (KMO) test of sampling adequacy (0.820) and Bartlett's test of sphericity (3099.65, p < .001), both indicating that the data set was appropriate for factor analysis. Factors were then extracted using a principal components analysis, and the final factor solution was rotated to a simple structure using varimax rotation. The outcome solution from the scree test indicated a two-factor model accounting for approximately 29% of the variance .... The authors assigned factor labels to reflect the item content, where Factor 1 was labelled 'attributions for positive outcomes' ... and Factor 2 was labelled 'attributions for negative outcomes'... . For both factors, low scores represent IC responses and high scores represent EU responses. (pp. 123–124)

If you have read this chapter, you should be able to understand this statement of the procedure which was applied, and the outcome of it.

FAQs

What is an eigenvalue?

An eigenvalue is the sum of the squared correlations between the variables and a factor. It can be used to decide how many factors to retain in the solution; factors with an eigenvalue greater than 1 may be retained. But some authorities dislike this criterion and suggest one should use the scree test to decide how many factors to retain.

What is a 'good' factor loading and what is not?

Some authorities recommend that if a factor loading (the correlation between a variable and a factor) is 0.3 or higher, the variable should be included as one of the measures of the factor and used in naming the factor. But there is no fixed criterion, and other authorities will use a higher one such as 0.4 or 0.5.

What is meant by rotating factors?

With just two factors, one can think of them as the axes of a two-dimensional graph with the variables plotted to show their loading on each of the factors. By rotating the factors about their common zero point, the loadings of the variables on each factor may be altered so that, for example, a particular variable comes to load more highly on one of the factors and less highly on the other. So rotating the factors can make the loadings of the variables less ambiguous and the interpretation of the factors easier. The basic idea applies with more than two factors (although it is harder to visualise).

SUMMARY

After reading this chapter you should be able to decide whether your data lends itself to factor analysis, interpret the output from principal components analysis, decide on the number of factors to extract, decide whether to request a rotated factor solution and interpret the output of factor analysis.

GLOSSARY

Oblique factors   factors which are correlated are sometimes said to be oblique, because if they were plotted the axes would not be at right angles.

Principal components   a version of factor analysis where the communalities in the correlation matrix are left at 1. Principal components analysis is usually performed as the first stage of a factor analysis.

Scree test   a plot of eigenvalues against components which can be used to determine how many factors to extract in a factor analysis.

REFERENCES

Bryman, A. and Cramer, D. (1997). *Quantitative Data Analysis with SPSS for Windows.* London: Routledge.

Child, D. (1990). *The Essentials of Factor Analysis.* London: Cassell.

Giles, D.C. (2002). *Advanced Research Methods in Psychology.* Hove: Routledge.

Grogan, S., Conner, M., Willits, D. and Norman, P. (1995). Development of a questionnaire to measure patients' satisfaction with general practitioners' services. *British Journal of General Practice*, 45, 525–529.

Grogan, S., Conner, M., Norman, P., Willits, D. and Porter, I. (2000). Validation of a questionnaire measuring patient satisfaction with general practitioner services. *Quality in Health Care*, 9, 210–215.

Harris, N. (2003). Reassessing the dimensionality of the moral emotions. *British Journal of Psychology*, 94, 457–473.

Kline, P. (1994). *An Easy Guide to Factor Analysis*. London: Routledge.

Silvester, J., Patterson, F. and Ferguson, E. (2003). Comparing two attributional models of job performance in retail sales: a field study. *Journal of Occupational and Organizational Psychology*, 76, 115–132.

Tabachnick, B.G. and Fidell, L.S. (1996). *Using Multivariate Statistics* (3rd edn). New York: HarperCollins.

Tabachnick, B.G. and Fidell, L.S. (2001). *Using Multivariate Statistics* (4th edn). Boston, MA: Allyn and Bacon.

7

Path Analysis

WHAT PATH ANALYSIS IS

Path analysis makes use of multiple regression analysis to look at the relationship between variables. The primary difference between the techniques is that path analysis graphically and explicitly looks at causal factors. The relationships between variables are designated by path coefficients (the standard regression coefficients from multiple regression) and show the effect of the independent on the dependent variables and also any relationships between independent variables.

INTRODUCTION TO PATH ANALYSIS

Sewell Wright, a geneticist, first published what developed into 'path analysis' in 1918. In essence, it visually (and statistically) separates out direct and indirect relationships between variables. Over a series of papers on the subject Wright further refined and developed the concept; the key paper entitled 'The method of path coefficients' was published in 1934. (The term 'coefficient' here refers to the regression coefficient from multiple regression analysis.) Path analysis became an important tool in population genetics, economics and, from the 1960s onward, the social sciences. Lately the technique has been applied to political trends and it can be used in any situation where regression would be used.

Allison (1999) suggests that path analysis is little more than the graphic illustration of multiple regression. This may be true; it is not a complicated technique. It is the graphic illustration, however, that adds richness to the data as it emerges through the diagramming process and leads to an end product that can clearly show relationships, strengths and directions.

Path analysis can be defined as a statistical technique which makes use of multiple regression to test causal relationships between variables. It is used not only to test causal relationships but also to ask questions about the minimum number of relationships (causal influences) and their directions; this is done by observing the sizes of the regression coefficients with and without certain variables entered into equations. Huang et al. (2002, p. 149) suggest that the 'goal of path analysis is to provide plausible explanations of observed correlations by constructing models of cause-and-effect relations'. This explanation brings together the key elements of path analysis: the idea that it is one way of constructing a model that, though based in statistical theory, is ultimately the expression of the researcher's creativity and ability to hypothesise and test relationships between variables. Note here that although you can test individual pathways using path analysis you cannot test the entire model with all of the pathways. To do that you need structural equation modelling (covered in chapter 8).

WHEN DO YOU NEED PATH ANALYSIS?

Path analysis is used when you have complex relationships between variables that may not be adequately examined using multiple regression analysis. You can use path analysis when you have developed a hypothesis about the causal relationships between variables, so it is applied when you are examining the sorts of relationships you might investigate using regression with more than one independent variable. There are, however, several crucial differences between path analysis and regression. The first is that there can be more than one dependent variable. The second is that the correlations between independent variables can be more readily accessed or identified.

Generally, once you have formed some hypothesis about which and in what manner variables may be related, you begin by constructing a path diagram. Path analysis is valuable when a visual representation of data aids in understanding the relationships it contains as it helps to identify and assess the significance of competing causal pathways.

WHAT KINDS OF DATA ARE NEEDED?

Path analysis uses the same types of data as multiple regression, but the number of variables can be expanded.

HOW MUCH DATA?

As in multiple regression, one needs a minimal amount of data. Authorities do not always agree, but generally 10 cases per variable is regarded as sufficient.

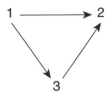

Figure 7.1(a)   Example of a path diagram

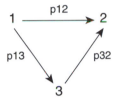

Figure 7.1(b)   Path diagram with path coefficients included

HOW DO YOU DO PATH ANALYSIS?

The first step is the construction of a path diagram to describe some hypothesis you have developed about your data. This hypothesis will be one that is explicit about causality.

The advantage of path analysis is that you can see which variables exert effects on others, whether these are direct or indirect and detect spurious paths. A direct effect is one between two variables with no intervening variable; indirect effects are those that are mediated through some intermediary variable. In Figure 7.1(a), variable 1 exerts a direct effect on variable 2. Variable 1 also exerts an indirect effect on 2 through variable 3. Note that variable 1 would be considered exogenous (there is no arrow pointing towards it) and variables 2 and 3 endogenous (both have arrows pointing towards them).

In Figure 7.1(b) the paths are specified and this could be considered an input diagram, the first stage in hypothesising the relationships between variables. The letter/number combinations represent the path coefficients and are quite basic with p12 designating the path between variables 1 and 2, p13 the path between 1 and 3 and p32 the path between 2 and 3.

Direct and indirect effects

Everitt and Dunn (2001) stress the importance of the technique as a way of testing assumptions about relationships. They observe that with the technique one can

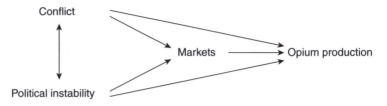

Figure 7.2(a) Path diagram for opium production

make distinctions between the direct, indirect and total effects of one variable on another, and define these effects:

> the direct effect is the influence of one variable on another that is not mediated by any other variable that is part of the model; the indirect effect is the effect of one variable on another that is mediated by, or passes through, at least one other variable in the system; and the total effect is the sum of the direct and indirect effects. (p. 292)

Figure 7.2 shows two simple path diagrams and explains the significance of arrows in showing direct and indirect effects. (Remember that the path diagram, where relationships are hypothesised but not yet quantified, is the first step in path analysis.) Opium production, according to the UN, has increased in the past several years. The reason for this has been related to conflict, political instability and markets. Figure 7.2 is concerned with how these variables might be related.

In Figure 7.2(a) the variables 'markets' and 'opium production' are endogenous variables since both have single-headed arrows pointing at them. Endogenous variables are variables explained by the model. 'Conflict' and 'political instability' are exogenous variables and have single-headed arrows pointing away from them and a double-headed arrow between them. The double-headed arrow linking 'conflict' and 'political instability' means that the variables are correlated. The single-headed arrows pointing away from 'conflict' and 'political instability' indicate direct and indirect effects: the single-headed arrows pointing at 'opium production' and 'markets' are direct effects. 'Conflict' and 'political instability' also exert an indirect effect on 'opium production' through their effect on 'markets'.

In Figure 7.2(b) the relationship between the variables has been changed. Here, 'conflict' and 'political instability' are uncorrelated and although both still exert indirect effects on 'opium production' through 'markets', only 'political instability' exerts a direct effect on 'opium production'. In Figure 7.2(a) only 'markets' and 'opium production' were endogenous variables; in Figure 7.2(b), 'conflict' is also an endogenous variable as indicated by the single-headed

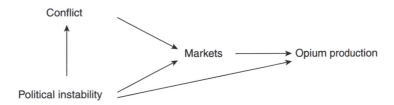

Figure 7.2(b)   Alternative path diagram for opium production

arrow pointing towards it. 'Political instability' is the only exogenous variable in Figure 7.2(b).

In both Figure 7.2(a) and (b), the models are said to be 'recursive', which in this context means that the effects are unidirectional. (The opposite is 'non-recursive', which would be exemplified by a feedback loop.) Path analysis usually tests models that are recursive, although with advanced software (LISREL, AMOS or EQS, for example) non-recursive models can be tested. (This is often done through structural equation modelling.)

CONVENTIONS

There are explicit conventions about how to draw path diagrams. These include the following:

1 Containers for the variables can be boxes, circles or ellipses as long as they are used consistently. (There are stricter rules which apply to structural equation modelling.) Some sources indicate specific purposes for each shape, but there is no rigid convention (and which shapes are used seems to depend on the researcher's computer skills).
2 A single-headed arrow is for the direct effect.
3 A double-headed arrow is for covariance between a pair of exogenous variables or between a pair of disturbances or errors. (This arrow is sometimes curved.)
4 The causal chain of effects is drawn from left to right.
5 Links between variables are indicated by single arrows from independent to dependent variables.

Huang et al. (2002) note that the path diagram can be constructed as follows:

6 A straight arrow is drawn to each output (endogenous) variable from each of its sources.
7 A straight arrow is also drawn to each output variable to indicate its residual (error).
8 A curved, double-headed arrow is drawn between each pair of input (exogenous) variables thought to have a non-zero correlation.

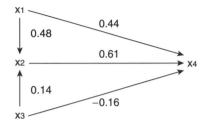

Figure 7.3 Example of path diagram with path coefficients

Other sources are in agreement with the use of arrows and their direction but frequently there is some confusion about whether the shape of the arrows should be altered to suggest the relative effect of that variable. For instance, one source suggests making arrows wider to suggest stronger relationships and another suggests using a dashed line to indicate a negative relationship. Whatever method you choose to use it is important to use it consistently. Path analysis is a way of ordering and visualising data and relationships between variables and though there are specific conventions as to single- or double-headed arrows it is a creative exercise, so some flexibility can be admitted.

ASSUMPTIONS

The assumptions of path analysis depend on the complexity of the model itself. The primary ones are: (1) The causal direction is one way. The arrows linking causes and effects proceed in one direction with no reciprocal or circular relationships. Another way to describe this is as a 'recursive model'. (2) Error terms (residuals) are not correlated. (3) The relationships between variables are linear and additive. (4) The sample size should be large enough to determine significance. So there should be at least 10 times as many cases as there are variables.

THE TOTAL EFFECT

Huang et al. (2002) use path analysis in the diagnosis of complex industrial processes. In their example they have four variables, x1, x2, x3 and x4, which are shown in Figure 7.3 with path coefficients.

Path coefficients are obtained by using multiple regression, regressing the endogenous variable(s) onto each of the variables that have an effect on it. In this example two standard multiple regression analyses need to be run: one with the variable x4 regressed onto x1, x2 and x3 and another with x2 regressed onto x1

Table 7.1   Total effects for the path shown in Figure 7.3

	x1	x2	x3
x4	0.73	0.61	− 0.07

and x3. Once this has been done, the direct effects, indirect effects and total effects can be assessed.

An important way to use the path model once it has been constructed and another way to look at the strength of individual paths is by determining the total effect. In this example we can find the total effect from x1 to x4 by summing the products of the direct and indirect effects. The path from x1 to x4 takes two routes. There is a direct effect from x1 with a coefficient of 0.44. There is also an indirect effect from x1 to x2 to x4. The strength of this indirect effect is calculated by multiplying the two relevant coefficients, 0.48 and 0.61, to give 0.29. The total effect of x1 on x4 is given by adding the direct and indirect effects, so in this case is 0.44 + 0.29 = 0.73.

Computing the total effect for x2 again means that we look at each path to x4 that x2 takes. As it only takes one, the total effect for x2 is simply 0.61.

From x3 the path is more complicated, with x3 going directly to x4 and then indirectly through x2. The total effect of x3 is the sum of the direct effect (−0.16) and the indirect effect via x2 (which is 0.14 × 0.61 = 0.09), so total effect for x3 is − 0.07.

A total effects table can be drawn up to summarise these total effects, as shown in Table 7.1. What we have found here is that the total effect of x1 to x4 is stronger than it appeared in the path model where the effect of x2 on x4 seemed the strongest. Computing the total effect may uncover relationships that are not immediately apparent; putting the information in the form of a path model allows it to be accessed more easily.

CALCULATION OF ERROR TERMS

To illustrate how to calculate error terms, we will follow the analysis of Farrell et al. (2004).

Type 1 diabetes (also called diabetes mellitus) is a condition in which the pancreas does not produce enough insulin. If the condition goes untreated there can be a variety of associated degenerative conditions such as progressive loss of sight and blood flow to the extremities. When someone has diabetes they need to administer insulin to themselves as well as adhere to a certain diet and exercise regimen (i.e. co-operate with treatment). Farrell et al. investigated 'the impact of cognitive disorders, stress and adherence on metabolic control in youths with type 1

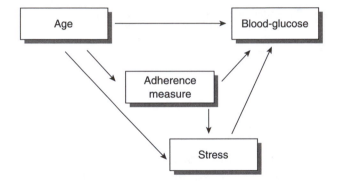

Figure 7.4 Example of initial path model

diabetes'. The focus here is on how a number of variables influence the ultimate blood-glucose levels. The variables used were: date of diagnosis, cognitive errors, life stressors, diabetes stress, adherence measure and blood-glucose. The authors state that because there had been no previous empirical data to favour any one relationship over another, they present their initial model as a 'completely identi-fied model', which means that every recursive path was explored. For simplicity, we will consider a simpler path model than that which the researchers developed. Here we will consider the variables age, adherence measure (amount of co-operation with treatment), stress and blood-glucose.

The initial path model based on hypothesised relationships between the variables is shown in Figure 7.4.

The next step is to use the data from the study to perform a regression analy-sis. In this case three separate regressions will be run. The first has blood-glucose as the dependent variable. With β representing the computed regression coeffi-cients, the regression equation represents the pathway:

$$\text{Blood-glucose} = \beta \text{ age} + \beta \text{ adherence measure} + \beta \text{ stress}$$

The regression for blood-glucose yields the following beta values:

Pathway between age and blood-glucose = 0.009
Pathway between adherence and blood-glucose = 0.410
Pathway between stress and blood-glucose = 0.520
R^2 is computed by SPSS to be .463.

For each regression analysis, R^2 is produced by the statistical software. There is often confusion here because R^2 is sometimes defined simply as the beta value squared. This is the case if there is one predictor variable (as we will see with adherence measures and age), but when there is more than one then R^2 is

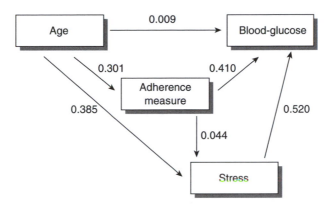

Figure 7.5 Path diagram showing regression coefficients

independently generated. (So if a report does not state the error, it cannot be found just from the path coefficients.)

The second analysis has stress as the dependent variable, so the regression equation is:

$$\text{Stress} = \beta \text{ age} + \beta \text{ adherence measure}$$

This second regression analysis yields the following beta values:

> Pathway between stress and age = 0.385
> Pathway between stress and adherence measure = 0.044
> R^2 is computed to be 0.170.

The third analysis has the adherence measure as the dependent variable, and the regression equation is:

$$\text{Adherence measure} = \beta \text{ age}$$

The third regression gives the beta value:

> Pathway between adherence and age = 0.301
> R^2 is computed to be 0.090. (In this case, with only one predictor
> variable, R^2 is simply the beta value squared.)

Inputting the beta values into the path diagram gives Figure 7.5.

The calculation of error requires a little bit of maths. Many texts skip over the process and logic of this step by saying simply that error is computed by the equation $1 - R^2$ where R^2 is simply the beta value squared. But this is not strictly accurate. Error is indeed determined by subtracting R^2 from 1, the 1 indicating the total variance in each endogenous variable. But as has been explained, it is not always the beta value squared.

Table 7.2   Error values for the variables in Figure 7.5

R^2 values		Calculated error
Blood-glucose	0.463	$1-R^2 = 0.537$
Stress	0.170	$1-R^2 = 0.830$
Adherence	0.090	$1-R^2 = 0.910$

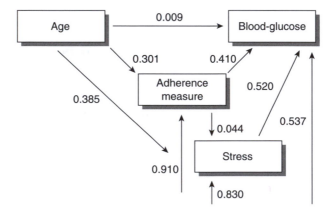

Figure 7.6   Path diagram showing regression coefficients and error terms

An R^2 value is determined for each of the dependent variables involved and then an error term can be computed for that variable. For example, in our first regression the direct pathways from the dependent variable (blood-glucose) were listed and the regression coefficients and R^2 determined. $1-R^2$ in this case is $1 - 0.463 = 0.537$ and so the error term associated with blood-glucose is 0.537.

The R^2 values from each of the regression coefficients of Figure 7.5 are listed in Table 7.2.

The calculated error is the variance that is left unaccounted for by the model. Error terms are usually displayed with an arrow pointing to the appropriate endogenous variables, that is the variables with arrow(s) pointing towards them, as shown in Figure 7.6. In this example they are 'blood-glucose', 'adherence measure' and 'stress'.

EXAMPLES FROM PSYCHOLOGY, HEALTH AND BUSINESS

From psychology

Barling et al. (1993) look at some of the enduring perceptions of working mothers and non-working mothers and the influence employment has on their young children. Questionnaires were distributed to mothers of 2- and 3-year-old children, who fell into three employment categories: 'full-time at home', 'paid employment outside the home for fewer than 10 hours per week' and 'looked after children while engaged in paid activity at home'. A total of 187 question-naires were usable. In their model, Barling et al. predicted that homemaker role experiences (skill use and role overload) would predict certain elements of well-being (positive or negative mood and cognitive difficulties) and that these, in turn, are related to parenting and child behaviour. Barling et al. first produced a model where all possible indirect and direct effects were included. Another model was then produced that excluded those paths that were not in their conceptual model (the hypothesised model). These models were then compared; it was found that because the model including all possible direct and indirect effects and the con-ceptual model were sufficiently similar, the conceptual model held and their hypothesis was supported. The key conclusion here was that it is not whether the homemaker works that contributes to positive mood and more positive child behaviours, but rather the ascribed role value: 'working' or 'non-working'.

From health

Path analysis is often used to assess multiple complex variables contributing to illness. Diabetes, as noted in a previous example, has complex causes and effects. Lustman et al. (2000) looked at how anti-depressants can help with depression related to diabetes. They demonstrate, using path analysis, that when depressed individuals with diabetes are given anti-depressants rather than a placebo they see an improvement in their diabetic status. This is because, Lustman et al. show, the relief in depressive symptoms causes an increased compliance with diabetes treatment. (It is notable that in this study path analysis is just one of a variety of statistical techniques employed. Reporting the results of a variety of techniques increases the strength of their account of what the data demonstrated.)

From business

Rucci and Sherman (1997) carried out a path analysis in looking at how employee and customer satisfaction is related to financial performance and were able to build a predictive model where these levels of satisfaction could predict financial performance. What was somewhat novel about the study was that the executives of the company developed what they felt, based on their experience, to be a causal model and then sent this to an econometrics firm which deter-mined the path coefficients and relative path strengths. The company was then able to make the appropriate adjustments to ensure better 'satisfaction' and thus increase profits.

FAQs

Path analysis is also called causal modelling and used the term causal several times, but you have also said that it is not a causal model, so which is it?

Although it is called a causal model it works on the assumption of causation, but this does not mean that it confirms causation. As with most calculations determined by multiple regression, they are predictions.

Can path analysis be used for exploratory rather than confirmatory purposes?

Path analysis is mainly for confirmatory purposes as some idea about the relationships between variables must exist before developing the model. Some sources do indicate that path analysis can be used for exploratory purposes, but the danger is that by developing endless numbers of path models without any clear idea about the relationship between variables, it is more likely that a model that seems significant will appear by chance.

How exactly can I compute path coefficients in SPSS?

Because path coefficients are the same as standard regression coefficients (betas) you can make the calculations in the same way as outlined in the chapter on multiple regression.

Some sources discuss 'model fit' – what is that and why isn't it covered here?

Model fit refers to a process that assesses how well the model represents the data and is more suitable for discussion in the chapter on structural equation modelling.

SUMMARY

Path analysis is a technique that exerts, in the words of one authority, 'an ordering effect on data'. It does this in several ways. Perhaps most important is the visual representation which is the path model. Its construction allows the researcher to see the relationships between variables that might not otherwise be revealed in the raw data.

The primary steps covered in a path analysis are:

1   The path diagram is hypothesised.
2   Direct and indirect effects are identified.
3   Starting with the variable furthest to the right, multiple regressions are run for each of the variables to which it is connected by a single-headed arrow.

4   If there are any double-headed arrows, the linear correlations between the variables linked by the double-headed arrow are calculated.

5   The residual variance is calculated.

Although many sources indicate that the relationships that are being looked for are 'causal', they do not really mean it! There is no causality here but there are strengths of relationships which can be compared, tested and refined. Furthermore, as Baron (2001) points out, path analysis (as with many techniques in this book) tells only part of the story about data. He suggests that although path analysis is a useful technique, it is best combined with other modes of explanation, and observes that in his area of interest understanding the genetic underpinning of complex disorders can be enhanced by using statistical techniques to supplement other types of information rather than in isolation.

GLOSSARY

Causal model   path models are sometimes called causal models because the causes and effects can be diagrammed. (However, it does not mean that the models actually demonstrate causality.)

Direct effect   the influence of one variable on another which is not mediated by any other variable that is part of the model.

Endogenous/exogenous variables   endo- is a prefix designating 'within'; exo-designates 'without' or 'outside'. Endogenous variables are explained by other endogenous and exogenous variables within the diagram. Endogenous variables will have a single-headed arrow pointed *at* them and are also the dependent variables. Exogenous variables have arrows pointing away from them and their values are taken as given by factors from 'outside' the model. These are usually independent variables.

Exogenous variables   see endogenous/exogenous variables.

Fully recursive   a fully recursive model has all paths specified.

Indirect effect   the effect of one variable on another that is mediated by, or passes through, at least one other variable in the system.

Input diagram   an input diagram is the first, hypothetical, diagram that is drawn where relationships may be specified to be positive or negative.

Non-recursive   non-recursive models are those that may contain arrows that loop or reverse direction; this type of model cannot be tested by regression.

Output diagrams   an output diagram is one where relationships have been computed and tested.

Recursive   a type of model where the causal flow goes in one way and is said to be 'unidirectional'. Not all the paths in this type of model have to be specified.

Residual effect (residual variance)   variance not explained by the model. It is represented as an external variable.

Standardised multiple regression coefficients   the standardised regression coefficients (also called beta weights) are the path coefficients and are calculated using regression analysis by regressing each variable onto every other variable to which it is connected by a path (arrow).

Total effect   the sum of the direct and indirect effects.

REFERENCES

Allison, P. (1999). *Multiple Regression: A primer*. London: Pine Forge Press.
Barling, J., MacEwan, K. and Nolte, M. (1993). Homemaker role experiences affect toddlers' behaviors via maternal well-being and parenting behavior. *Journal of Abnormal Child Psychology*, 21, 213–229.
Baron, M. (2001). The search for complex disease genes: fault by linkage or fault by association? *Molecular Psychiatry*, 6(2), 143–149.
Everitt, B. and Dunn, G. (2001). *Applied Multivariate Data Analysis*. London: Edward Arnold.
Farrell, S., Hains, A., Davies, W., Smith, P. and Parton, D. (2004). The impact of cognitive distortions, stress, and adherence on metabolic control in youths with type 1 diabetes. *Journal of Adolescent Health*, 34, 461–467.
Huang, B., Thornhill, N., Shah, S. and Shook, D. (2002). Path analysis for process troubleshooting. Proceedings of Advanced Control of Industrial Processes, Kumamoto, Japan, 10–12 June, 149–154.
Lustman, P., Freedland, K., Griffith, L. and Clouse, R. (2000). Fluoxetine for depression in diabetes. *Diabetes Care*, 23, 618–623.
Rucci, A. and Sherman, S. (1997). Bringing Sears into the New World. *Fortune Magazine*, 13 October.

FURTHER READING

Bryman, A. and Cramer, D. (1990). *Quantitative Data Analysis for Social Scientists*. London: Routledge.
Shipley, B. (2002). *Cause and Correlation in Biology: A User's Guide to Path Analysis, Structural Equations and Causal Inference*. Cambridge: Cambridge University Press.
Waller, N. and Meehl, P. (2002). Risky tests, verisimilitude, and path analysis. *Psychological Methods*, 7, 323–337.

8

Structural Equation Modelling

WHAT STRUCTURAL EQUATION MODELLING IS

Structural equation modelling is a confirmatory, multivariate technique that looks at causal relationships between variables in a diagrammatic form. An advancement of path analysis, structural equation modelling is a process of model development that looks at the relationships between observed and latent variables where the goal is to select a model that best accounts for the data. Structural equation modelling is almost exclusively a computerised process and is used extensively in the social sciences, economics, population genetics, marketing, ecology and other fields where the analysis of complex data sets can be used to make educated guesses about behaviour – human, market or otherwise.

INTRODUCTION TO STRUCTURAL EQUATION MODELLING

Path analysis, which is described in an earlier chapter, is a method of organising and illustrating relationships in data which make it easier to comprehend or 'see' relationships compared with portraying similar information in a matrix, where links may not be immediately obvious. To test hypotheses about data, each pathway in the model is determined through multiple regression and then various direct and indirect effects described. The resulting path diagram or 'model' demonstrates the significance (or spuriousness) of the various paths. Path analysis allows path coefficients (the relationship between variables) to be determined, but there is no way to test the entire model. Additionally, path analysis requires recursivity (that the path direction is one way with no feedback loops), which may be restrictive for some studies.

Structural equation modelling (also called covariance structure models) addresses both of these limitations. It is essentially a development of path analysis which allows you not only to develop path diagrams but also to perform tests to see which has the best 'fit'. Structural equation modelling (SEM), like path analysis, is used extensively in the social sciences, economics and other fields where a number of complex relationships must be examined efficiently. As a multivariate technique, it takes account of a number of variables at the same time and helps to measure what we cannot see based on what we can. In the case of SEM, what we can 'see' and measure directly are called (unsurprisingly) observed variables, and what we have not measured directly are referred to as latent variables.

Latent variables are often theoretical constructs like 'liberalism' or 'conservatism'. We cannot observe liberalism or conservatism or measure them directly. We can, however, assume that the concepts of liberal or conservative have various constituents that we can measure. We could look at voting behaviour, views on certain issues, socio-economic status, education level and type, geographical area or any number of measurable variables that could effect the characterisation of liberal or conservative.

SEM can be done by hand and there is a set of statistical equations that are associated with the technique, but it was only with the advent of the computer and a particular program that the technique became feasible for working with a significant number of variables. The program, called LISREL (LInear Structural RELations), was developed by Jöreskog (1973) with the intent to 'derive causal inferences using data originating from non-experimental research' (Saris, 1999, p. 220). In this chapter we will discuss the general logic of the approach and some of the associated computer programs and types of output generated from them.

The actual 'structural equations' that underlie the procedure are sets of equations which are developed to explain relationships before the model is analysed. These are derived from the path model or from the path model's resulting matrix, but for the purposes of this explanation this will not be discussed as the task is performed by the relevant computer programs. (The mathematically curious may like to refer to Everitt and Dunn, 2001, pp. 291–307.)

The key element of SEM is the estimation of the effects of latent variables (variables you cannot see) on the observed variables in your path diagram. MacLean and Gray (1998) say the way this works is that: 'SEM assumes there is a causal structure among a set of latent variables, and that the observed variables are indicators of the latent variables. The latent variables may appear as linear combinations of observed variables, or they may be intervening variables in a causal chain' (p. 2). Although the word causal has been mentioned here, it is more or less a convention and the models do *not* indicate causality. Rather, they suggest possibilities based on the assumptions they make about the data set.

SEM utilises a mixture composed of an essence of the general linear model, dollops of factor analysis, a sprig of path analysis, grated multiple regression and other techniques from the statistical kitchen all included in statistical packages that assess complex, multivariate relationships in data.

WHEN DO YOU NEED SEM?

SEM is applied to situations where a number of variables are present and uses many of the statistical techniques discussed elsewhere in this book. It is not a statistical technique itself but rather a collection of techniques pulled together to provide an account of complex patterns in the data. It is especially useful in the social sciences and psychology where 'concepts' (latents) are frequently encountered. Concepts such as intelligence, empathy, aggression or anxiety are often subjects of analysis; each of these is defined with respect to observed as well as other latent variables. What is important is that latent variables are unobserved and only understood through their relationship to each other and to observed variables. SEM seeks to understand the relationships between latent variables and the observed variables which form the structural framework from which they are derived. It also allows for these relationships to be proposed as predictive models.

There is nothing new in SEM: most of the techniques are well known and used, but it combines them and adds the spin of a visual component to aid in the assessment of complex data.

WHAT KINDS OF DATA ARE NEEDED?

Generally, SEM is appropriate for multivariate analysis of qualitative and quantitative data. Large sample sizes ($n \geq 200$ observations and usually many more) should be used, but it really depends on the number of variables. Most sources recommend 15 cases per predictor as a general rule of thumb for deciding what is the minimum size of a data set. But these are only rules of thumb: the number of observations in SEM is dependent on how many variables there are. There is a simple formula that dictates this: number of observations = $[k(k + 1)]/2$ where k is the number of variables in the model.

HOW DO YOU DO SEM?

As noted above, the technique is a computer-driven one, so in this section the basic logic and order in which steps of the procedure are carried out will be explained, and an overview of computer programs that handle SEM provided.

Kenny (1997) divides the procedure into four steps but we shall add a further step to the process. The steps are: specification, identification, estimation and testing of model fit. Stage 1, specification, is a statement of the theoretical model in terms of equations or a diagram. Stage 2, identification, is when the model can, in theory, be estimated with the observed data. Stage 3, estimation, is when the model's parameters are statistically estimated from data. Multiple regression is one method of estimating parameters, but more complicated methods are often used. In stage 4, testing of model fit, the estimated model parameters are used to predict the correlations or covariances between measured variables. The predicted correlations or covariances are compared with the observed correlations or covariances, and the amount of agreement is assessed.

Kelloway (1998) cites previous sources in adding 'respecification' to the list. This may be the last step required if the model does not fit the data and has to be modified. (This usually involves deleting non-significant paths and may (or may not) lead to a better model fit.)

Specification

This step is constructing the path diagram which is the researcher's hypothesis about the relationship between variables. (An example is shown in Figure 8.1 below.) It is often not based on experiment or empirical observations but is a creative process mediated through previous research, experience with the topic at hand or even, as Kelloway (1998, p. 7) points out, a hunch. In this step the researcher will determine how the latent variables will be measured (usually with four or more indicators).

Although usually taken care of by the computer programs, there is technically a limit to the number of paths that can be analysed in a model, say Norman and Streiner (2003), and this number is contingent on a number of other elements. They further indicate that 'the number of parameters must be less than or equal to the number of observations' (p. 161). The number of parameters is determined by adding the following terms:

    the number of paths;
    the number of variances of exogenous variables;
    the number of covariances;
    the number of disturbance (error) terms.

As in path analysis, there are exogenous and endogenous components to the diagram. Endogenous variables are explained by other endogenous and exogenous variables within the diagram. They have a single-headed arrow pointed at them and are dependent variables. Exogenous variables have arrows pointing away from them and their values are taken as given by factors from 'outside' the model. Independent variables are exogenous variables, but not all exogenous variables are independent variables since latent variables can include endogenous and exogenous variables. But this can be tricky to understand with all this jargon. First, a latent variable is one that is not directly measured (as in the example of the concepts of liberalism or conservatism mentioned earlier). If an endogenous

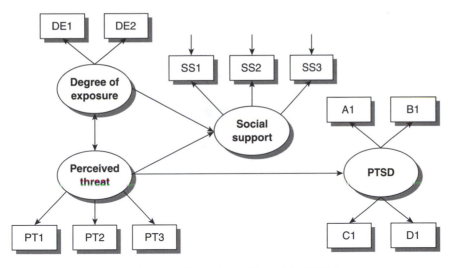

Figure 8.1 An adaptation of King and King's (1997) model of PTSD

or exogenous variable is not directly measured by the researcher, then it can be considered a latent variable. Exogenous variables may not seem to fit here. But recall that although they are generally independent (and thus not determined by other variables in the model), they can be correlated with other variables.

SEM is concerned with examining models of the relationships between the endogenous and exogenous variables. A model can be thought of as 'a set of theoretical propositions that link the exogenous variables to the endogenous variables and the endogenous variables to one another' (Kelloway, 1998, p. 8).

The way the arrows in a diagram such as Fig 8.1 are used translates directly from path analysis, with single-headed arrows designating direct effects of a variable and double-headed arrows demonstrating correlation between two variables. But in SEM there are stricter conventions about the specific geometric forms by which variables are represented. For example, in the model shown in Figure 8.1 which has been adapted from King and King (1997), the latent and observed variables relating to post-traumatic stress disorder (PTSD) are considered. PTSD is an important example because in its clinical characterisation it is explicit about contributing elements being other latents that can be assessed by specific observable variables such as stress scales and other measures. Each computer program that deals with SEM is slightly different and has different ways of organising the diagram – the example shown in Figure 8.1 is a generic one and includes the standard conventions such as designating latent variables with ellipses, observed variables with rectangles and error terms with free script (i.e. without a container) or within circles.

In the model shown in Figure 8.1, degree of exposure is correlated with perceived threat, and this is indicated by the double-headed arrow. The variables in rectangular boxes are the variables that we can measure and are hypothesised to underlie the latent variables in the model. The model here seems 'busy' with arrows, boxes and ellipses but there is a good reason for this: SEM makes the assumption that all causes are represented in the model, so it is important to have a fairly good idea about the relationships you think might exist.

Error terms and disturbance terms (which are the same thing) are also important considerations in the specification of the model. Error terms are associated with the observed or measured variables. In regression there is an assumption that there is zero measurement error, but SEM specifically takes into account these error terms. Why? Because the error terms, if not accounted for in this way, result in a bias of the path coefficients.

To sum up, the specification of a model is the graphical explanation of hunches, theory, experience, design and creativity formed into a structural model.

Identification

Identification of a model is about finding a solution for the model. Sometimes there is one unique solution but often there are a number of possible solutions from which one must be selected. Identification involves 'the estimation of unknown parameters (e.g., factor loadings or path coefficients) based on observed covariances/correlations' (Kelloway, 1998, p. 14).

There are three basic types of solution for models and these solutions refer to each parameter estimate: just-identified, under-identified and over-identified:

1   In a just-identified model there is a single unique solution (solution here means a set of path values) for each parameter estimate. This is a model that is a perfect fit and in reality does not seem to occur all that often.
2   Under-identified refers to models where there are an infinite number of parameter estimates and thus any reliable solution becomes a remote possibility. Often sources use the analogy of having an equation like $a + b = 12$. There are infinite possibilities of what a and b could be.
3   Over-identified models are those that have a number of solutions but a single 'best' solution. Working with over-identified models is generally preferred.

Estimation

Assuming an over-identified model, LISREL, EQS, MX, AMOS or any number of SEM computer programs estimate model parameters. (They do this by comparing the implied covariance matrix with the observed covariance matrix again and again until they arrive at a position where the two are very similar.) This takes place 'behind the scenes' during the running of the program. It is primarily maximum likelihood and ordinary least squares that are used for the estimation of these parameters (for a full explanation of these techniques see Everitt and Dunn, 2001, pp. 173–211).

Model fit

LISREL and other programs do this process automatically, so the important issue here is how to interpret and assess what the computer outputs for model fit are saying.

Each type of program gives similar indications of fit but varies in the number of measures it provides in the output: LISREL will have 15 and AMOS up to 25 different measures. (The measures included in a report of the outcome should be limited so it does not appear as if you are just throwing in everything in the hope that some are good indicators.) Because each program provides so many indices of fit we will discuss fit generally in terms of absolute, comparative and parsimonious fit. Some specific tests are mentioned; this is not a complete list of tests available, but indicates those which are most commonly used.

Absolute fit is where the model developed replicates the actual covariance matrix. In the programs available this measure is determined by a number of indices. (Because each program, as mentioned, differs in what it reports in its output, only the key indices will be listed here.) For absolute fit the main indices are: goodness-of-fit index (GFI), adjusted goodness-of-fit index (AGFI), root mean squared residual (RMR) and root mean squared error of approximations (RMSEA).

Goodness-of-fit indices ranges from 0 to 1 and, according to Kelloway (1998, p. 27), values exceeding 0.9 indicate a good fit. He goes on to caution, however, that this is based on experience and should not be taken as an absolute.

Adjusted goodness of fit is differentiated from regular goodness of fit in that it adjusts for degrees of freedom in the particular model. The range for AGFI is also 0 to 1, with values larger than 0.9 indicating a good fit.

Root mean squared residual (RMR) is calculated from the residuals and ranges from 0 to 1 with a significantly good fit indicated if the value is less than 0.05 (Byrne, 1998). This figure of 0.05 is similar to a typical 'significance level' but is not the same. The RMR and others discussed here are their own indices and 0.05 or under is an indicator, not a significance level.

Root mean square error of approximation (RMSEA) is a measure of fit that 'could be expected if the model were estimated from the entire population, not just the samples drawn for estimation' (Zhang, 2001). As with RMR, the indicator that a reasonable goodness of fit has been found is when the value is less than 0.05.

Comparative or relative fit refers to a situation where two or more models are compared to see which one provides the best fit to the data. One of the models will be the total independence or null hypothesis model where there is known to be a poor fit. The comparative fit index (CFI) is the primary measurement here and ranges from 0 to 1 with values above 0.9 considered to indicate a good fit. The non-normed fit index (NNFI) is similar to the Tucker Lewis index (which is another index of fit indication measured on the same scale and which may also be encountered as a test) and has a range of 0 to 1 with values approaching 1 indicating a better fit. The non-normed fit index (and the associated normed fit index (NFI)) are fairly robust measures unless the sample size is small (small here meaning less than the recommended sample size of over 200), in which case the result can be difficult to interpret.

Parsimonious fit is about finding a balance between adding more parameters to give a better fit and shaving these parameters for better statistical validity. Kelloway (1998, p. 10) indicates that 'the most parsimonious diagram [is one that] (a) fully explains why variables are correlated and (b) can be justified on theoretical grounds'. Parsimonious normed fit indices and parsimonious goodness of fit have ranges 0 to 1, with results approaching 1 (0.90 or higher) indicating a parsimonious fit.

The Akaike information criterion is another measure of fit but does not conform to the ranges that we have seen here. It compares models and generates a numerical value for each model; whichever has the lower number is the better fit. These numbers can often be in the hundreds so appear strange in the context of the much smaller numerical values used in many of the other indices.

SOME COMPUTER PROGRAMS

LISREL was the first and some argue is still the best program for SEM. It is now more user-friendly than it used to be although it still requires some basic programming skills. Currently, student versions can be downloaded free from the website: www.ssicentral.com. The handbook to use the program is included on the website. (The program is an execution (.exe) type file, which may be an issue for those working on networked university systems where downloading such files is forbidden.)

MX is an SEM program which does what it needs to do in a no-frills way. It is free to download and fairly easy to use. Like LISREL, the download is an .exe file.

SPSS has not yet released its own SEM program but does exclusively distribute AMOS. AMOS is window based, easy to use and generates elegant diagrams. AMOS and SPSS are compatible so you can transfer data sets from SPSS to AMOS.

EQS is a Windows-based program with all the bells and whistles one could hope for. It is easy to use and the diagrams are easily and intuitively developed.

EXAMPLES OF SEM

From psychology

Twin studies have long been a mainstay in psychology and have allowed researchers to examine whether certain pathologies are related to heredity (or not). In an example from physiological psychology, Hulshoff-Pol et al. (2002) adapt SEM to look at differences in brain structure amongst twins and singletons. The authors state that SEM was selected to test assumptions about aspects of twin versus singleton brain physiology (with the null hypothesis being that there is no difference). The physiology was measured using a variety of indicators, including percentages of different types of brain matter and relative volumes. (There were dozens of variables.) The latent variables in this study were 'genetic influences'. The observed variables were the measurable physiologies such as brain volume, volumes of the ventricles and other measures determined by MRI scan.

Hulshoff-Pol et al.'s results suggest that although there is some evidence to support the idea that second-born twins have slightly less intra-cranial volume, the overall development of grey and white brain matter does not differ in twins and singletons.

From health

Bollen and Schwing (1987) explored the relationship between air pollution and mortality using SEM. They noted that much of the previous research exploring this relationship used regression analysis and did not take into account the error associated with measuring pollution. This problem seems well suited to the application of SEM, with 'pollution' being a latent variable that is characterised by any number of observable or measurable phenomena.

Bollen and Schwing found that by including error (which was not previously taken into consideration) and using SEM, a more serious picture emerges with respect to the relationship between mortality and air pollution. Using a well-know air-pollution model they added plausible error measurements. This resulted in a huge increase in the estimated effect of air pollution. They caution that the results are experimental and not meant to imply that the models were intentionally inaccurate, but that by using different methods, like SEM, more accurate modelling of pollution effects can be performed.

From business/management

One important area of business in which SEM is used is in market research. Here, researchers must try to predict buying behaviours based on a number of observable characteristics. SEM is appropriate as it can take into account a number of variables and uncover the significance of latent (unobserved) variables.

A summary of how SEM is applied in market research can be found in MacLean and Gray (1998). One example they describe is concerned with predicting the purchase of overseas holidays by Japanese single women (so-called OLs, which is short for Office Ladies), who have more disposable income than most others in the working population. They identified certain relevant factors including fashion consciousness, assertiveness, materialism, conservatism and hedonism. These are all latent variables; they cannot be assessed directly but can be understood through a number of indicators. A number of questions were developed to assess the identified latent variables. For example, hedonism was assessed by requiring a yes/no answer to statements such as 'I want to enjoy the present rather than think about the future'.

Path diagrams were then constructed based on the results. The authors concluded that by identifying, quantifying and diagramming the relationships between observed and latent variables, predictions could be made concerning how this group made decisions to make purchases. In this case the decisions were about whether or not this group was likely to purchase holidays, and it was found that fashion consciousness and hedonism were the best predictors of purchasing an overseas holiday.

FAQs

When a model is said to fit does that mean it is the solution?

No, when a model fits it is not 'accepted' as such but is rather the model that most closely approximates the associated matrices.

What about missing data?

If missing data is present most of the programs mentioned will automatically apply maximum likelihood estimation to make best use of the data available.

What is the difference between latent variables in SEM and factors in factor analysis?

They are very similar and both are functions of measured variables. SEM utilises factor analysis in preliminary analysis.

SUMMARY

Structural equation modelling (SEM) is a more structured and formalised incarnation of path analysis yet retains flexibility and depends on the researchers' critical thinking. Although much of the work in SEM is now done by computer programs, it is still up to the researcher to decide if the representation of the data is accurate (or elegant).

Latent variables form the real basis of SEM and are similar to factors. They are not 'real' but often these implied variables are of great importance. To develop a model and have it achieve a balanced fit can have real impact on research, but such a model should not be taken as truth but rather a possibility.

GLOSSARY

Fit this is how well the model ultimately represents the associated statistical matrices. In structural equation modelling this is done 'behind the scenes' with the primary job of the researcher being to interpret the outputs. Fit can be determined in a number of ways with perfect fit being achieved at the expense of statistical power. (The converse is also true, and a balance is what is aimed for.)

Model this is the researcher's theory about the relationships between variables. Usually it is not based on experiment but on experience, research or, as some indicate, hunches or common sense.

Latent variable an unobserved variable that may be correlated with other latent variables but is underpinned by measured or observed variables.

REFERENCES

Bollen, K. and Schwing, R. (1987). Air pollution-mortality models: a demonstration of the effects of measurement error. *Quality and Quantity*, 21, 37–48.

Byrne, B. (1998). *Structural Equation Modeling with LISREL, PRELIS, and SIMPLIS: Basic Concepts, Applications and Programming*. Hillsdale, NJ: Lawrence Erlbaum.

Everitt, B. and Dunn, G. (2001). *Applied Multivariate Data Analysis*. London: Edward Arnold.

Hulshoff-Pol, H., Posthuma, D., Baaré, W., De Geus, E., Schnack, H., van Haren, N., van Oel, C., Kahn, R. and Boomsma, D. (2002). Twin-singleton differences in brain structure using structural equation modelling. *Brain*, 125, 384–390.

Jöreskog, K. (1973). A general method for estimating a linear structural equation. In A. Goldberger and O. Duncan (eds), *Structural Equation Models in the Social Sciences*. New York: Seminar Press.

Kelloway, E. (1998). *Using LISREL for Structural Equation Modeling: A Researcher's Guide*. London: Sage.

Kenny, D. (1997). Terminology and basics of SEM. http://www.nai.net/~dakenny/basics.htm. Accessed 22 November 2003.

King, D. and King, L. (1997). A brief introduction to structural equation modeling. *PTSD Research Quarterly*, 8, 1–4.

MacLean, S. and Gray, K. (1998). Structural equation modelling in market research. *Journal of the Australian Market Research Society*, 6(1). http://www.smallwaters.com/whitepapers/. Retrieved 2 September 2004.

Norman, G. and Streiner, D. (2003). *PDQ Statistics*. (3rd edn). Hamilton, Ontario: B.C. Decker.

Saris, W. (1999). Structural equation modelling. In H. Ader and G. Mellenbergh, *Research Methodology in the Social Behavioural and Life Sciences*. London: Sage.

Zhang, Z. (2001). *Implementation of Total Quality Management: An Empirical Study of Chinese Manufacturing Firms*. Rijksuniversiteit Groningen: Labryint.

FURTHER READING

Bollen, K. (1989). *Structural Equations with Latent Variables*. New York: Wiley.

Hoyle, R. (1995). *Structural Equation Modeling: Concepts, Issues and Applications*. London: Sage.

Kline, R. (1998). *Principles and Practice of Structural Equation Modeling*. New York: Guilford Press.

Loehlin, J. (1993). *Latent Variable Models: An Introduction to Factor, Path and Structural Analysis*. Hillsdale, NJ: Lawrence Erlbaum.

INTERNET SOURCES

www.utexas.edu/its/rc/tutorials/stat/amos/
Provides an excellent overview of SEM and AMOS.

www2.chass.ncsu.edu/garson/pa765/structur.htm
A good overview with links to other SEM sites.

www.gsu.edu/~mkteer/semnet.html
Access to SEMNET, an SEM chat room and discussion forum.

9

Time Series Analysis

WHAT TIME SERIES ANALYSIS IS

Time series analysis (TSA) examines the trends in repeated observations taken over time intervals, usually with equal intervals between them. The research questions addressed by TSA are concerned with changes in the observations over time and the 'shape' (either increase or decrease, sharply or gradually) of these changes. The changes are broken down into three possible components: a trend over time, a seasonal trend and changes due to random fluctuations. TSA can be used to examine such issues as the effect of an intervention (such as a drug treatment programme on drug consumption), the influence of an environmental change uncontrolled by the researcher (such as a sudden change in the price of drugs), and to develop equations from available data to predict future occurrences under similar circumstances. The numerous research questions which TSA can address are indicated by the variety of areas in which the technique is used, which include business, economics, manufacturing, social sciences, functional imaging.

TSA is a complex and highly specialised technique. We shall only attempt to provide a broad outline of what it does and how it does it.

WHEN DO YOU NEED TSA?

In TSA the dependent variable comprises observations taken on a number of occasions separated by time. For example, the observations could be questionnaire data, measures of quality control, the value of share prices: any variable which is expected to change as a result of the passing of time or the occurrence of some event. TSA can address three types of research question: (1) Are there patterns in a data series taken over time? (2) Does an independent variable have an impact on the dependent variable measured over the time series? (3) Can an equation be produced which will effectively forecast (predict) future observations?

A simple example illustrates the potential application of TSA in determining the impact of an event (a 'broken' time series). Thioridazine (used to treat schizophrenia and related psychoses) was reported to lead to ventricular arrhythmias by the Committee for Safety of Medicines in December 2000. Wright et al. (2004) investigated whether this announcement had any effect on the prescribing of antipsychotic medication. They obtained information about the number of prescriptions and amount spent on antipsychotic medication from five primary health care trusts for 19 months prior to the announcement and 16 months following it. Their results demonstrated that there was a drop in the prescribing of thioridazine after the announcement and an increase in the prescribing of alternative antipsychotic medications. They concluded that the advice given by the Committee for Safety of Medicines had affected doctors' prescribing behaviour.

TYPES OF TSA RESEARCH DESIGNS

Simple time series design

This, the most common time series design, consists of quantitative measures taken over regular time points, usually by the repetition of surveys or some other quantitative data collection. An example of a simple time series is the collection of unemployment figures on a quarterly or yearly basis.

Cohort analysis design

This involves the study of a group of people who have lived through a particularly significant event and have experienced the event at approximately the same time. In a cohort study design, the individuals examined over time may not be the same but they should be representative of a particular group (or cohort) of individuals who have shared a common experience. When cohort analysis design is used, a table is constructed to display the results with columns for the time intervals of data collection (the survey interval) and rows for the groups in the data (the cohort interval), for example age groups such as 15–20 years, 21–25 years, etc.

Panel studies design

A panel study design is similar to a cohort design except that the same individuals are followed up over the time intervals. In this way the participants act as their own controls (as in many repeated measures designs). However, participants who are examined over repeated time points may be affected by having previously completed the measures being used. (This is known as sensitisation.)

Therefore, it is sometimes necessary to include a control group matched on age and gender with which to compare the panel group at each time interval.

Event-history design

This is a 'catch-all' term and refers to a group of techniques used within TSA. The events which are of interest to the researcher (e.g. start of menstruation in adolescent girls, reoccurrence of a depressive episode) may not take place at the same time and so the time when an event occurs is of interest too. Event-history designs can form part of a panel study design, but the data collected usually refers to organisational behaviour rather than individuals.

DIFFERENT TYPES OF TSA

Spectral analysis

Spectral or Fourier series analysis converts the plot of the dependent variable over time into its sine and cosine wave components to produce a sum or integral of these functions and examines the degree to which the plot differs from the sine or cosine waveforms. The breakdown of a dependent variable into sine and cosine waves makes interpretation of the results more difficult for the non-mathematician and spectral analysis is generally used in mathematics, theoretical physics and other traditional sciences. The statistical packages currently available are not able to analyse multivariate time series data with spectral analysis and this restricts its value for the social sciences where greater use is made of time domain analysis.

An example of spectral analysis in animal sciences is provided by Kuwahara et al. (2004) who used it to examine the effect of housing on the variability and diurnal rhythms of the heart rates of six miniature swine. The animals were housed first of all individually, then in pairs for three weeks and finally were returned to individual housing. Electrocardiograms (ECGs) were used to examine the heart rates of the animals and these were compared during the different housing conditions. The authors report that when the swine were housed in pairs, heart rate increased but returned to baseline levels within two weeks. Kuwahara et al. concluded that housing animals in pairs has a positive effect on heart rate and adaptation to environmental changes in swine appears to take approximately two weeks.

Time domain analysis

Time domain analysis uses the raw dependent variable directly rather than converting the scores in the manner found in spectral analysis. This eases the interpretation of the results and also makes the technique generally more accessible to non-mathematicians. Time domain analysis is the technique most widely used in social science research.

Forecasting

Forecasting is not a distinct type of TSA but a way in which the results from TSA can be used. It is frequently used in economics, often in conjunction with regression analysis. Data can only be predicted from a time series model which explains the data reliably, so it is important that the sample of respondents used and the time series data are representative of the population from which they are drawn. Even so, caution is needed since future data can only be predicted if the circumstances are similar to those which existed when the original data was collected. In areas such as economics this is not so much of a problem: changes occur slowly and the factors which determine them are relatively fixed and readily observable. However, in the social and biomedical sciences there are numerous factors which affect the dependent variable. Some of these (such as changing socio-political climate) are not under the control of the researcher and are not necessarily made explicit at the point of data collection. Although prediction is possible from TSA, it needs to be treated with caution and the constraints of the initial data need to be made explicit.

Statistical packages offer prediction from TSA analysis and will generate confidence intervals within which the results can be considered reliable. (Confidence intervals provide the upper and lower bounds within which the predicted score may actually be located, so that with 95% confidence limits you can be 95% confident that the predicted score will be within them. The wider the confidence intervals, the less reliable the results, since the upper and lower bounds of the possible scores are further apart.)

Pereira (2004) offers an example of the use of forecasting in health care management. Maintaining the correct amount of blood available for transfusion is becoming a growing problem, especially with the reduction in the number of people willing to donate blood. Pereira used TSA to develop a model to predict the amount of blood that would be needed for future transfusions at a university hospital in Barcelona. The time series data comprised the required blood from January 1988 to December 2002 from the Hospital Clinic Blood Bank and the time series was divided into two, the 'older' and the 'younger'. The older time series was used to generate the model and the younger was used to test the accuracy of the predictions of the model. The time series model was used to forecast demand for the years 2000, 2001 and 2002, using three different procedures: an ARIMA model, an exponential smoothing model and neural network architecture (these are different ways of making predictions). The observed and the forecasted data are displayed in Figure 9.1, from Pereira's paper. The distance

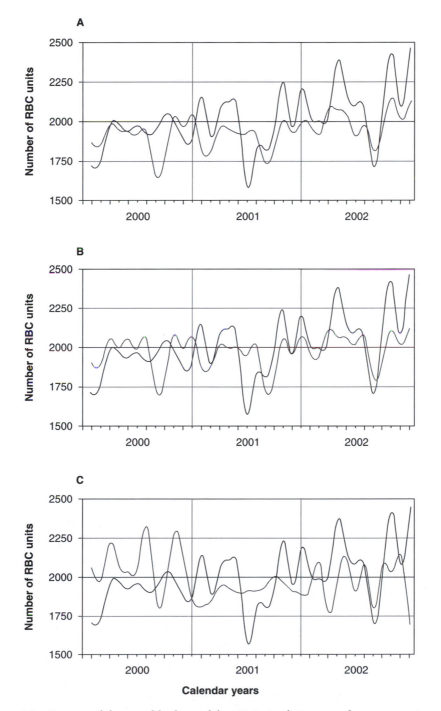

Figure 9.1 Forecast of the monthly demand for RBC transfusion over three consecutive one-year horizons. Observed values (black line) and those forecasted (grey line) by ARIMA (A), exponential smoothing (B) or neural-network-based models (From Pereira, 2004, p. 745)

between the actual values and the predicted ones is a measure of the amount of error in the model. Pereira concluded that both the ARIMA and exponential smoothing models were able to predict the amount of blood needed for transfusions within certain limits, demonstrating their usefulness as a predictive tool.

WHAT KINDS OF DATA ARE NEEDED?

Any data where the same observations are made over a period of time on the same individuals can be analysed using TSA as long as the dependent variable meets the parametric requirements of homogeneity of variance and normality. The dependent variable observations are taken at different times which are usually equidistant (e.g. hourly, daily, monthly or yearly). TSA is an extension of the general linear model, and therefore the changes over time in the dependent variable are thought to be linear in nature. (There are TSA methods which can cope with a curvilinear trend in the dependent variable but they are not covered here.) Generally, a minimum of 50 dependent variable observations over time is required.

HOW YOU DO TSA

TSA uses a number of technical terms, and this can make it difficult to follow. At the end of this chapter there is a list of frequently used terms specific to TSA which may assist you to understand the technique. The mathematical equations behind TSA are very complex so TSA is only used when statistical packages are available.

TSA starts with a set of data which can be plotted against time, and the aim is to reveal the underlying trends, express these in equations (which form a model of the data) and possibly generate predictions based on the model. A number of models can be used, some of which are linear and some non-linear. The linear models include auto-regressive (AR), moving average (MA) and the combination which is both auto-regressive and moving average (ARMA). Non-linear models include threshold auto-regressive (TAR), exponential auto-regressive (EXPAR), auto-regressive conditional heteroscedastic (ARCH) and others. The most frequently used model is the auto-regressive, integrated, moving average (ARIMA) model, also referred to as the Box–Jenkins model. It has three parameters, p, d and q, which are set at values (usually 0, 1 or 2) such that the model summarises the data as accurately as possible. The researcher enters the values of p, d and q into the computer program, and it is therefore necessary for you to understand what each of these values means and represents in terms of the data you have used.

There are three main phases in the analysis: identification, estimation and diagnosis. The three phases of TSA are performed in one analysis session. The results from the analysis are then considered by the researcher in terms of their reliability in explaining the data. If changes are required to improve the results the values of p, d and q are altered accordingly and the analysis rerun until the time series model produced adequately explains the fluctuations in the dependent variable over time.

In the identification phase, the analysis examines the degree to which the data is stationary (whether the mean and variance in the dependent variable is constant over time). If it is not stationary, the data is 'differenced' to remove any trends and the number of times this has to be done is expressed in the d parameter of the ARIMA model. Differencing the dependent variable means that the earlier scores are subtracted from later ones, that is observation 1 is subtracted from observation 2.

Determining the number of times which a data set needs differencing can be achieved by examining a graph of the dependent variable scores over the time course: the degree to which the mean changes over time determines the number of times the data needs to be differenced. The optimal level of differencing is the one which produces the smallest standard deviation in the dependent variable over time. If over-differencing occurs, the value of d is set too high and this can obscure other trends in the data set. Over-differencing can be detected from a plot of the autocorrelation functions (ACFs) or the residuals. The ACF plot is a graph showing the autocorrelations for the dependent variable observations over time, while the residual plot is a graph of the residual values which are left after the time series has been modelled. If over-differencing has occurred, the ACF plot shows a spike in the autocorrelations, while in the residual plot the data points will alternate between being positive and negative.

If no differencing is required, d is 0. When d is 1, linear trends have been removed to make the data set stationary. Plotting the lag 1 scores (i.e. the scores for where observation 1 has been subtracted from observation 2 etc.) against time should produce a line which is approximately horizontal if the mean has been made stationary over time. If it is not, a d of 2 may be required to remove both linear and quadratic trends. The scores at the appropriate lags are used in subsequent calculations.

In the second phase of the analysis, the parameters in the model are estimated. The plots of the ACFs and the partial ACFs (PACFs) are used to assess the size of the p and q values. The value of the parameter p is the autoregressive element of the ARIMA, which means it represents the number of correlations needed to model the relationship between the observations; that is, whether one observation has an effect on the value of successive observations. When p has a value of 1 there are correlations between the values at lag 1; when it is 2 there are correlations between the values at lag 2.

The value of q in the ARIMA model is the moving average component; it represents the relationship between the current score and the random shocks at previous lags. When q is 1 there is a relationship between the current scores and the random shocks at lag 1; if q is 2 there is a relationship between the current score and the random shocks at lag 2. As with d, when either p or q are 0 they are not needed to model the data in a representative manner.

When estimating the p and q values there are a few rules which apply. The technicalities are more complex than can be covered here, but two points worth making are that the parameters included all differ significantly from 0 or they would be excluded from the model and both the auto-regressive and moving average components are correlations and as such will be between −1 and +1.

The changes or cycles in the ACFs and PACFs can be either local, which means weekly or monthly patterns in the data, or seasonal. An example of a seasonal cycle is the fluctuation in Christmas tree sales, which increase steadily towards the middle of December compared with a low baseline throughout the remainder of the year.

Using the ARIMA model, the components would be presented in this manner: $(p,d,q)(P,D,Q)_s$, with the first brackets containing the model for the non-seasonal aspect of the time series, the second brackets containing the components necessary to model the seasonal component and the subscript s indicating the lag at which the seasonal component occurs.

Random shocks are unpredictable variations in the dependent variable. They should be normally distributed with a mean of zero. The influence of random shocks is important for both the identification and estimation phases of TSA: in the identification phase they are sorted and assessed; in the estimation phase the size of the ACFs and the PACFs is used to reduce the random shocks to their normally distributed (and random) state, effectively removing any pattern. The residuals plotted in the diagnostic phase of the analysis reflect the random shocks in the data set.

Pereira's (2004) ACF and PACF plots of the time series before and after differencing can be seen in Figure 9.2. The background to the study, as mentioned earlier, was the need to model demand for blood in a hospital clinic. The A and B parts of Figure 9.2 represent the original time series. Pereira reported that there was a significant trend in the ACF up to Lag 16. This can be in Figure 9.2A as the reasonably steady decline in the ACF through to Lag 16. The data was differenced once to remove a linear trend and this led to the PACF decreasing exponentially (see Figure 9.2D) and left a spike in the ACF data at Lag 1 (seen in Figure 9.2C). 'In both correlograms [i.e. Figure 9.2A and B] there is a significant positive coefficient at Lag 12, which … supports the presence of seasonal effects with a 12-month period' (p. 742). On the basis of these plots the ARIMA model thought to fit the data adequately was $(0,1,1)(0,1,1)_{12}$.

In the third phase of the analysis, diagnosis, the model produced by the estimation phase is assessed to see whether it accounts for all the patterns in the dependent variable. During the diagnosis phase, the residuals are examined to

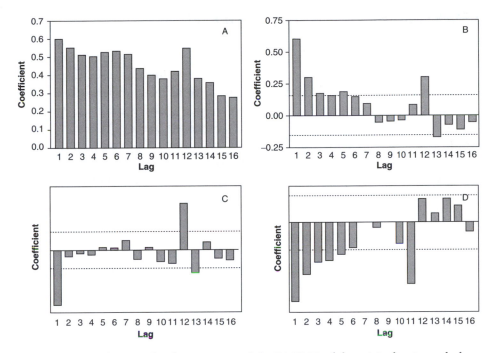

Figure 9.2 Correlograms for the ACF (A) and the PACF (B) of the original series and after one-pass differencing (C and D, respectively). Dotted lines represent the significance level (From Periera, 2004, p. 5)

determine the effectiveness of the model which has been developed. The residual plots illustrate the difference between the data predicted by the model and the actual data. Periera (2004) illustrates this procedure: 'Graphical analysis of residuals displayed no obvious trend ... . values of residuals did not significantly deviate from a normal distribution with a mean of zero .... This confirmed that the selected ARIMA model gives an accurate representation of the time series' (p. 742).

There are two measures of goodness of fit produced for TSA: the root mean square residual (RMS) and R^2. RMS is a measure of the squared residuals over time and as such does not directly take into account the dependent variable. The smaller the RMS value, the smaller the amount of error present and the more accurate the fit of the model to the data. R^2, the most frequently used goodness-of-fit measure, determines the amount of variance explained by a model.

To compare the goodness of fit of two different ARIMA models, the Akaike information criterion (AIC) can be used if the two models are related (or 'nested') to one another (e.g. ARIMA (0,1,0) compared with ARIMA (1,1,0)); to compare models which do not have any common elements, the Schwarz Bayesian criterion (SBC) can be used. With either measure, the general aim is to produce criteria which are as small as possible.

ASSESSING THE EFFECTS OF AN INTERVENTION

An independent variable can be introduced into the analysis to determine the effect which an intervention has on the time series within a data set. Usually, the situations which give rise to TSA can be classified as quasi-experimental situations where the researcher has control over when the intervention is introduced (and it may be introduced more than once). Since the onset of the intervention tends to be under the control of the researcher, the duration for which the effect of the intervention lasts is the variable of interest.

In principle, the analysis is simple: the time series before and after the intervention are compared for any differences. The three phases of identification, estimation and diagnosis are performed for the observations prior to the onset of the intervention, then the onset of the intervention and its duration are included and the model rerun. Coefficient values for the post-intervention period are found and compared with those before the intervention to determine whether the intervention has had a significant impact on the time series.

The effect of the intervention may be either abrupt or gradual and it may have a permanent or temporary effect. This means that there are four possible combinations of effect and duration. In time series jargon, an intervention which has abrupt onset and a temporary duration is referred to as an impulse intervention, while an intervention which has an abrupt impact and permanent effects is referred to as a step function.

The relationship between the impact of an intervention and its duration is referred to as a transfer function. The two parameters which comprise the transfer function contribute to an equation which determines the degree of change in a time series as a result of the intervention. The two components are: the length of time taken for the post-intervention time series to return to its pre-intervention pattern (δ), and the amount of change in the post-intervention series compared with pre-intervention time series (ω). The degree to which these values differ significantly from 0 is tested. When ω is 0, there is no effect of the intervention; when ω is significantly different from 0, it indicates the size of the change in the time series. The value of δ varies between 0 and 1. When it is 0, there is an abrupt impact of the intervention; as the value of δ reaches 1, the onset of change in the post-intervention time series is more gradual. The extent of the impact of the intervention is indicated by the regression coefficient (B).

MULTIVARIATE TSA

The multivariate form of TSA can include multiple dependent variables, allowing the comparison of one time series with another or the inclusion of a covariate in the model. The comparison of two different time series is also referred to as cross-correlation function, transfer function model, models with input series and dynamic regression.

When a covariate is included, both the dependent variable and covariate are modelled (after the effects of random error have been removed), and then the degree of similarity between the models for the dependent variable and covariate are assessed. There are not many examples of multivariate time series to be found in the published literature (TSA is complicated enough without making it multivariate!). However, Miwakeichi et al. (2004) used a multivariate auto-regressive model to determine the foci of epileptic seizures in five unilateral focal patients and one bilateral focal patient. They were interested in the (ECoG electrocorticogram) impulse response frequencies during sleep in epileptics and recorded ECoG response frequencies in each patient during normal sleep. The recordings were divided up into three-second epochs and for each patient the time series models were estimated separately for the left and right hemispheres. Results were compared during REM (Rapid Eye Movement), non-REM and the waking stages of sleep. From the ECoG results an attenuation function (whether there was a significant spike in a given brain area, larger than those reported across the whole brain, during a specific time point) was calculated for each epoch which was either positive or negative depending on the presence or absence of ECoG fluctuations. Miwakeichi et al. reported that in those patients with unilateral focal epilepsy the average attenuation coefficient was significantly larger (and showed greater variation) in the focal hemisphere, regardless of the phase of sleep. In the patient with bilateral focal epilepsy there was no difference between the hemispheres during the different phases of sleep or overall. The authors also report that for those with focal epilepsy there are larger attenuation coefficients during REM sleep when compared with non-REM sleep. The authors conclude that the multivariate auto-regressive model is a useful tool for the modelling of dynamic processes in the brain. Although their sample size was small, they had over 9000 observations for each patient which ensured that the time series model was sufficiently robust.

EXAMPLE OF TSA RESEARCH

From health

One example of environmental influence on human behaviour is the seasonal effect reported in both births and abortions. Weerasinghe et al. (2003) present time series data of the births and abortions for New South Wales, Australia, using data from 1989 to 1999. They examined the rates of births, voluntary abortions and non-voluntary abortions (miscarriages or spontaneous abortions). As the data was skewed, the median births/abortions for each month were used in the analysis.

The authors report that the proportions of births were highest in March, September and October and at their lowest in February and November. In order to examine whether the pattern of voluntary and non-voluntary abortions differed between those who were married or not, the data for these two groups was analysed separately. For married women, there were higher rates of voluntary abortion in February, and lower ones in April and June. There were proportionately more non-voluntary abortions in February and March. In women who had never been married, there was seasonality in voluntary abortions but not for non-voluntary abortions. The authors concluded that their data was similar to previous studies in showing that women are more likely to fall pregnant during the summer months. Although they concluded that temperature did not appear to be an influential factor in either birth or abortions, the reasons behind the seasonal trends in births and abortions could not be ascertained.

FAQs

What does the analysis really tell you that would not learn from examining graphical depictions of trends over time?

Through analysing graphs of dependent variables taken over it is possible to gain an appreciation of any trend (either increasing or decreasing) in the dependent variables. However, TSA determines whether these changes are large enough to be statistically significant. Additionally, it allows for independent variables and multiple dependent variables to be considered in terms of their statistical difference from one another. This is not detectable just by analysing graphical interpretations of the data.

Why does TSA place an emphasis on having sufficient observations over time rather than sample size?

The analysis is concerned with changes in scores over time. To model these changes reliably there need to be a representative number of measurements taken over a time course. TSA requires 50 or more observations to be available for analysis in order for the results to be considered a reliable and valid representation of the sample being tested.

SUMMARY

Time series analysis (TSA) examines the trends in repeated observations taken over time intervals, and is concerned with changes in the observations over time and the 'shape' of these changes. Time domain analysis, which uses the raw dependent variable scores, is the technique most widely used in social science research.

TSA starts with data which can be plotted against time, and aims to reveal the underlying trends and express these in equations which form a model. A number of models can be used, some linear and some non-linear.

The analysis has three main phases: identification, where the analysis examines the degree to which the data is stationary; estimation, where the parameters of the model are estimated; and diagnosis, where the model produced by the estimation phase is assessed through a consideration of the difference between the data predicted by the model and the actual data.

GLOSSARY

ACF autocorrelation function, the correlation between two scores which succeed one another in the time series.

ARIMA auto-regressive, integrated, moving average model (p,d,q).

d the trend or integrated element in the ARIMA model, which can be linear or quadratic.

Impulse intervention an intervention which has an abrupt onset and temporary effects on the time series. It is also known as a pulse indicator.

Indicator variable the variable which codes the onset and duration of an intervention.

Lag the differencing points in the time series. There is always one less lag than the number of data points when the data is differenced once, and when the data is differenced twice (lag 2) there are two less time points. The lags are calculated by examining the difference between successive time points, for example the second time point minus the first, the third time point minus the second.

p the effect of previous scores and the auto-regressive element in the ARIMA model.

PACF partial autocorrelation functions, the correlation between scores at alternate time points, with the middle time point being controlled for.

q the effects of the random shocks and the moving average element in the ARIMA model.

Random shocks random elements in the data, similar to error terms in other types of analysis.

Seasonal component where changes in the time series occur over a yearly basis. Its components are identified by capital letters in the ARIMA notation, with the lag at which it occurs indicated afterwards. Tends to be easily predicted over a time course and readily observable.

Sequence plot   the raw data of the dependent variable plotted over time.

Spectral analysis   (also known as Fourier analysis) This method breaks down the time series dependent variable into its sine wave components. This method is more frequently used in the traditional science areas.

Step function   an intervention which has an abrupt impact and a permanent effect.

Time domain analysis   the model of time series analysis most frequently used in social sciences, which handles the dependent variable directly and can be used to investigate interventions in time series data.

Transfer function   the relationship between an intervention and the effect it has.

REFERENCES

Kuwahara, M., Tsujino, Y., Tsubone, H., Kumagai, E., Tsutsumi, H. and Tanigawa, M. (2004). Effects of pair housing on diurnal rhythms of heart rate and heart rate variability in miniature swine. *Experimental Animals*, 53, 303–309.

Miwakeichi, F., Galka, A., Uchida, S., Arakaki, H., Hirai, N., Nishida, M., Maehara, T., Kawai, K., Sunaga, S. and Shimizu, H. (2004). Impulse response function based on multivariate AR model can differentiate focal hemisphere in temporal lobe epilepsy. *Epilepsy Research*, 61, 73–87.

Pereira, A. (2004). Performance of time series methods in forecasting the demand for red blood cell transfusion. *Transfusion*, 44, 739–746.

Weerasinghe, D.P. and MacIntyre, C.R. (2003). Seasonality of births and abortions in New South Wales, Australia. *Medical Science Monitor*, 9 (12), 534–540.

Wright, N.M., Roberts, A.J., Allgar, V.L., Tompkins, C.N., Greenwood, D.C. and Laurence, G. (2004). Impact of the CSM advice on thioridazine on general practitioner prescribing behaviour in Leeds: time series analysis. *British Journal of General Practice*, 54, 370–373.

FURTHER READING

Brokwell, P.J. and Davis, R.A. (2002). *Introduction to Time Series and Forecasting*. London: Springer.

Chatfield, C. (2003). *The Analysis of Time Series: An Introduction*. Boca Raton, FL: Chapman and Hall/CRC Press.

Christensen, R. (2001). *Advanced Linear Modeling: Multivariate, Time Series, and Spatial Data; Nonparametric Regression and Response Surface Maximization*. New York: Springer.

Kendall, M. and Ord, J.K. (1990). *Time Series* (3rd edn). London: Edward Arnold.

Nelson, B.K. (1998). Statistical methodology: V. Time series analysis using autoregressive integrated moving average (ARIMA) models. *Academic Emergency Medicine*, 5, 739–744.

Priestley, M.B. (1996). *Spectral Analysis and Time Series*. San Diego, CA: Academic Press.

INTERNET SOURCES

www.itl.nist.gov/div898/handbook/pmc/section4/pmc4.htm
www2.chass.ncsu.edu/garson/
www.abs.gov.au/websitedbs/
www.statsoftinc.com/textbook/

10

Facet Theory and Smallest Space Analysis

WHAT FACET THEORY AND SMALLEST SPACE ANALYSIS ARE

Facet theory and smallest space analysis together form a research package. Facet theory is a way of developing, organising and performing qualitative research. Smallest space analysis is similar to factor and principal components analysis but the output is visual: concepts are represented in physical space, with those more closely correlated closer together in geometric space.

INTRODUCTION TO FACET THEORY AND SMALLEST SPACE ANALYSIS

Facet theory, in essence, is a response to one of the primary concerns of most positivist research: the reliability and repeatability of experiments. In social sciences there needs to be flexibility, however, and positivist techniques are often misapplied. So how can one be scientific yet flexible? In the 1950s Louis Guttman and others working at the University of Jerusalem devised a technique that allows for some reconciliation of this tension. (Some authors indicate that it was in response to the limitations of factor analysis that they sought to develop the technique.) The technique is called facet theory and is concerned with systematising the way in which theory is constructed and research carried out.

Shye et al. (1994) sum up the purpose of facet theory by saying that it is concerned with 'the discovery of structural lawfulness'. This 'structural lawfulness' pertains to each area of facet theory. Guttman and Greenbaum (1998) identify five primary areas of the technique: theory construction, research design, choice of observations, data analysis, interpretation. These are not necessarily separate areas and each informs the other to some extent. If structural lawfulness can be developed for each area, we can begin to approach a system that is at once scientific and flexible. This system, facet theory, could be thought of as almost a 'research package', offering help with organisation and interpretation at each stage in a structured research process.

Facet theory is not really a statistical technique in the sense that others in this book are, although smallest space analysis does make use of the information developed through facet theory and can employ statistical techniques to construct its analyses.

Smallest space analysis is an adjunct to facet theory and can in some cases quantify the results. It falls under the 'data analysis' part of the five primary areas mentioned above. Though quantitative in nature (and the equivalent of factor analysis), smallest space analysis is a very visual and creative technique that complements the idea of 'structural lawfulness'.

WHAT KINDS OF QUESTIONS DO THEY ANSWER?

This question is a difficult one to apply to these techniques as they offer more of a total research package approach to the development, execution and analysis of a study. The answer to the question is a circular one: the types of questions that the researcher decides to ask of them. Facet theory allows for the formalisation of the research process and offers a structured approach to developing questions for research through the 'mapping sentence'. This mapping sentence will be discussed at greater length below, but in essence it is a technique for translating observations into research questions and design. Smallest space analysis is also a technique that evades the question. It is used for the visual representation of data derived through the use of facet theory. This is another somewhat circular answer and reflects the difficulty in characterising the technique as belonging to traditional statistics, but it also demonstrates the close relationship between facet theory and smallest space analysis.

WHAT TYPES OF PROBLEMS ARE THEY APPLIED TO?

Perhaps the most important type of problem or research challenge would be the example of raw data in the form of interviews and general theory about your chosen subject area. This can be developed in a systematic way by using facet theory and then analysed using smallest space analysis (SSA).

It is easier to characterise the sorts of problems that SSA is applied to because they are so similar to those that concern factor analysis, namely the assessment of scales of attitude, intelligence or political beliefs, using categorical (often ordinal) data. The difference is how data is represented: in factor analysis data is represented numerically while in SSA it is represented visually. As Guttman and Greenbaum (1998, p. 18) suggest, '[SSA] provides a geometric representation of intercorrelations among variables as points in Euclidean space. The distances between pairs of points in the space correspond to the correlations among the variables.'

WHAT KINDS OF DATA ARE NEEDED?

The raw data can be quantitative or qualitative depending on the sort of enquiry carried out. The data that is generated by the process of facet theory, which involves the production of structured research questions and methods, can be quantitative or qualitative. The data is transformed by the process of facet theory (the evolution of the mapping sentence) into discrete data – usually nominal or ordinal. It is at the stage when the data has been transformed that it can then be analysed using SSA.

HOW DO YOU USE FACET THEORY AND DO SSA?

Theory construction: the mapping sentence

The mapping sentence allows the researcher to conceptualise and design an experiment or research enquiry. The mapping sentence is the key element for this stage in the research, although just one element in the system or package that is built on the systematic deployment of elements.

For Guttman and Greenbaum (1998, p. 15), the task of the mapping sentence is to 'express observations in a form that facilitates theory construction in an explicit and systematic way'. But what exactly is it? The mapping sentence is a formalised way of asking a question that 'maps' onto the observations made in a piece of research. The word 'maps' here means exactly what it would in a geographical sense. Landforms, roads and towns have observed characteristics that are represented by maps and the mapping sentence represents a similar situation where the observed characteristics of a social phenomenon (for example) are represented in the sentence.

The mapping sentence is composed of a focus set and a sense set, together called the domain. The set of images, items, experiences, etc., to which the domain refers is called the range. Together, the focus, sense and range are called the universe of observations. To explain this we will work through an example.

Suppose we have a man named Robert and we make a statement about him: 'Robert eats apples.' The focus here is Robert – he is an element in a set of, say, all the men working at the BBC or all the men watching a musical. Suppose this set includes the elements Robert, Reginald, Roderick and Rudi. The sense set in 'Robert eats apples' is the word 'eats'. Eats is a member of a set of actions that might include eats, peels, throws, picks and shines. The image set in 'Robert eats apples' is 'apples'; we could say that this might include different types of fruit like pears or bananas, but in this case we will be more specific and say that it includes specific types of apples. The image set here is the 'range' and the range of apples might include Pink Lady, Granny Smith, Braeburn and Red Delicious. If we now put together these components we will have something that looks like the following:

Focus	Sense		Image
{Robert}	{eats}		{Pink Lady}
{Reginald}	{peels}	→	{Granny Smith}
{Roderick}	{throws}		{Braeburn}
{Rudi}	{picks}		{Red Delicious}
	{shines}		

This basic mapping framework, where we have the focus set and sense set making up the domain and the image set making up the range, is the general form of the mapping sentence. The arrow here, from domain to range, means that sets forming the domain are assigned (generally) to sets in the range. But like the adage 'the map is not the terrain', the mapping sentence does not designate what the actual assignment might be.

From this framework we can ask questions based on the structure. For example, we can ask: What sort of apple does Robert throw? Rudi eats what sort of apple? Which type of apple is peeled by Reginald? In this example there can be 20 such questions (the four men and the five actions). The focus set and sense set form a Cartesian set, which can be combined in 20 ways: Robert eats, Robert peels, Robert throws, …, Rudi shines. The objects of these actions are in the range and are the types of apples, so we might have Robert eats Braeburn [apples].

Further refining our vocabulary here we can say that the objects, people, items, concepts, etc., that make up the sense set and focus set, in addition to being components of a Cartesian set, are called a facet.

The above example can be expanded when we think about the everyday actions of men towards apples: Robert may eat any number of a variety of apples and Rudi may throw any sort that he can lay his hands on. To designate this relationship, we specify the image (or apple) set by putting double vertical lines around them. This allows for the explicit possibility of these choices, and when so designated is called a power set.

Focus	Sense		Image
{Robert}	{eats}		‖Pink Lady‖
{Reginald}	{peels}	→	‖Granny Smith‖
{Roderick}	{throws}		‖Braeburn‖
{Rudi}	{picks}		‖Red Delicious‖
	{shines}		

The double vertical lines also suggest that the set contains all the possible subsets, for example: (1) Pink Lady, Granny Smith, Braeburn, Red Delicious; (2) Pink Lady, Granny Smith, Braeburn; (3) Pink Lady, etc. Also we could say that the men commit actions against nothing: Robert throws nothing, for example. So {nothing} is also part of the set.

Staying with this example we might observe the following interactions of man and apple. (Note that the arrow is now double stemmed, indicating specific assignment):

Robert shines	⇒	{Pink Lady, Red Delicious}
Robert peels	⇒	{Granny Smith}
Robert eats	⇒	{Granny Smith, Pink Lady}
Reginald throws	⇒	{nothing}

Now we can further refine this design such that the range can be designated as a set of four {yes, no} facets which will refer to the varieties of apples present:

Focus	Sense		Image (the observed actions of men towards apples)
{Robert}	{eats}		
{Reginald}	{peels}	→	{yes, no} {yes, no} {yes, no} {yes, no}
{Roderick}	{throws}		
{Rudi}	{picks}		
	{shines}		

The power set has been transformed into {yes, no} sets called the 'range facets'. In the above illustration, note that the arrow is once again single stemmed: this is to designate not specific assignment but that these are all the assignments available.

Specific assignments might look like this:

Robert shines	⇒	[Pink Lady:] yes; [Granny Smith:] no
Robert peels	⇒	[Granny Smith:] yes
Robert eats	⇒	[nothing:] no; [Braeburn:] no

In this example we have constructed a type of mapping sentence that has as possible responses only 'yes' and 'no'. If, however, our empirical observations of the research subject (here the action of men towards apples) are different, then facet theory allows for the flexible refinement of the range.

Let us add another dimension to the range, and ask how often Robert eats apples: is it often, sometimes, rarely or never? We can now combine the previous range with the domain to refine our new range as shown in this diagram:

Domain		**Range**	
{Robert}	{eats}	{Pink Lady}	{often}
{Reginald}	{peels}	{Granny Smith} →	{sometimes}
{Roderick}	{throws}	{Braeburn}	{rarely}
{Rudi}	{picks}	{Red Delicious}	{never}
	{shines}		

In this mapping sentence, we can begin to see the structure of a questionnaire taking shape. We could assign numeric values (e.g. 1,2,3,4) to the range set and thus be able to score the sentences later. The mapping sentence is flexible enough at this stage to take into account new observations; in the above example, these concern the frequency of actions towards apples.

So far we have covered the construction of the mapping framework and sentence and explained that it is composed of a focus and sense that make up the domain and an image, experience or concept that make up the range. Symbols such as a single- or double-stemmed arrow have been described, as has the significance of double vertical lines around the range. Perhaps most important for this chapter on facet theory is the identification of the term 'facet' as it applies to the components of the sets.

There can be a variety of facets to both the domain and range. For example, with both there can be more than one facet and these can be very specific. First we will look at the 'range facet'. Taking a new example where we look at the performance of students in an exam, the mapping sentence might look like this:

Focus	**Sense**	**range[1]**	**range[2]**
{Jean}	{studied for}	{2–4 days}	{excellent}
{Mark}	{performed} →	{1–2 days}	{good}
{Guy}		{0–1 day}	{fair}
			{poor}

What is notable here is that the limits of the range suggest that they have come from empirical observation: they are not set arbitrarily, although they could be in the initial stages of development. The range could also be set at a more refined level which might indicate more precisely the hours studied or the exact percentage correct scored in the exam. The determination of the range is up to the researcher and depends on what is being looked at. The construction of the mapping sentence is a feedback mechanism between the actual construction and empirical observation.

The domain facets can be similarly expanded. According to Shye et al. (1994) there are two main ways that this can be done: extension and intension. In expanding the range facets we were concerned with the observed, and with the domain, the concern is in expanding the observations themselves. In the example Jean, Mark and Guy might be students at a college in Wolverhampton; applying extension, we might increase this population to include all the students at college in Wolverhampton.

Intension would, instead of expanding an existing facet, add a new one such that in the above example where the exam subject is not specified we might add history, philosophy, psychology, literature and mechanics. If both of these were applied, our example could look like this:

College student exams {history}   {studied for} {3–4 days} {excellent}
in Wolverhampton   {philosophy}   {performed}→ {1–2 days} {good}
                       {psychology}   {0–1 day} {fair}
                       {literature}   {poor}
                       {mechanics}

If we then did the study and gathered data for this example, the next stage might be assigning numerical values to each of the range facets – maybe 1–3 for R1 (1 = {3–4 days}, 2 = {1–2 days}, 3 = {0 days}) and 1–4 for R2 (1 = {excellent}, 2 = {good}, 3 = {fair}, 4 = {poor}). We could, after recording the scores that each student obtained in the exams after certain periods of study, organise a data matrix as in Table 10.1 below.

Before we talk any more about the data matrix, it is important that we move on to SSA because this is where the tools for looking at this data can be found. Again, this highlights the reliance of each methodology on the other as part of a total research package.

Data analysis using SSA

SSA – like many techniques in this book – involves the assessment and interpretation of multivariate data. In the case of SSA the data can be qualitative or quantitative. SSA is the geometric transformation of statistical meaning to concrete representation.

SSA is a way to represent multivariate quantitative or qualitative data graphically such that variables sharing a close relationship (determined by correlation or, in some cases, the 'opinion of experts') will appear closer as points in a field. Shye et al. (1994, p. 100) note that one advantage of using SSA is that 'picturing a multivariate concept as a physical space is an efficient way to tackle its complexity for theoretical and measurement purposes' and that by 'proposing a measure of proximity between two items, the investigator determines the nature of the conceptual proximity with which he or she is concerned ... the nature of this proximity, in turn, determines the structure of the concept as a behavioural system'. What this suggests is that the model which is created can then be used not only in the research experiment at hand, but also to provide structure for the concept under investigation. The key proponent and developer of facet theory, Louis Guttman, was also involved in circumplex-style diagrammings of intelligence and attitudes which were popular in the 1960s. SSA is explicitly used in conjunction with facet theory though it is often now used alongside techniques such as multidimensional scaling (MDS) and partial-order scalogram analysis (POSA). (For more on MDS and POSA, see Young and Hamer, 1987.)

The mapping sentence takes on a more concrete function in that elements from the universe of the mapping sentence are 'mapped' onto the physical, geometric space of the smallest space diagram. The smallest space diagram is referred to as such because it aims to represent information in the space that, according to Shye et al. (1994), 'has the lowest dimensionality' (p. 104) so that the parameters of the model can be restricted. (This is a sort of spatial Ockham's razor.)

So how are the proximities between items determined? The answer is by measures of similarity or a similarity index. Factor analysis is one of three ways by which such a similarity index can be constructed. (Factor analysis is concerned with correlations between variables.) In other cases, when the data is primarily qualitative and the concentration is on the closeness of 'meanings' rather than quantitatively derived numbers, the proximities of points are determined by a panel of judges.

SSA is most often carried out using a computer program that creates the graphical representation for you. Here we will go through a hypothetical example to demonstrate the basic logic of the procedure.

We will concentrate on an example which uses correlations. In the data matrix obtained from the mapping sentences involving Wolverhampton students, we had a scenario in which values had been assigned to each of the range facets: 3 for R1 (1 = {3–4 days}, 2 = {1–2 days}, 3 = {0 days}) and 1–4 for R2 (1 = {excellent}, 2 = {good}, 3 = {fair}, 4 = {poor}). We will look only at those students who studied for the maximum number of days (1={3–4 days}), and see what the relationships between the subjects might be. For this group of students, will good scores in history and philosophy be correlated with good scores in mechanics? Hypothetical data is shown in Table 10.1.

The hypothetical sample of students yields the imaginary correlational matrix (obtained from factor analysis procedures) shown in Table 10.2.

To build a smallest space diagram we start with the two variables with the lowest correlation: they will be represented as having the largest space between

Table 10.1 Hypothetical data of student performance in different exams

Student	Studied	History	Philosophy	Psychology	Literature	Mechanics
1	2	3	2	3	2	4
2	2	3	3	4	2	2
3	3	3	3	2	3	3
4	1	2	2	1	2	2
5	1	3	2	2	2	4
6	1	3	3	3	3	2
7	1	2	1	3	3	1
8	2	3	2	2	2	2
9	1	2	1	1	3	1
10	2	1	3	2	3	2

Table 10.2 Hypothetical correlation matrix of examination performance

	History	Philosophy	Psychology	Literature	Mechanics
History	1.000	0.199	0.373	0.447	0.519
Philosophy	0.199	1.000	0.200	0.000	0.319
Psychology	0.373	0.200	1.000	0.000	0.025
Literature	0.447	0.000	0.000	1.000	0.498
Mechanics	0.519	0.319	0.025	0.498	1.000

Figure 10.1   SSA diagram stage 1

them and are presented in Figure 10.1. This echoes the basic statement of Shye et al. (1994, p. 125) that 'the greater the similarity between two items, the smaller the distance between their respective points'.

Next we begin to add variables according to how they are related – mechanics is correlated with both philosophy and literature but has a higher correlation with literature and thus will be shown closer to literature, as in Figure 10.2.

As we continue building the model we will add psychology – but where can it go graphically? It has zero correlation with literature so it must be portrayed as distant, and a weak correlation with mechanics so it must be relatively far from that. It is somewhat correlated with philosophy and a not-as-yet-added history. So our best guess at this point would put it near but not too close to philosophy, as in Figure 10.3.

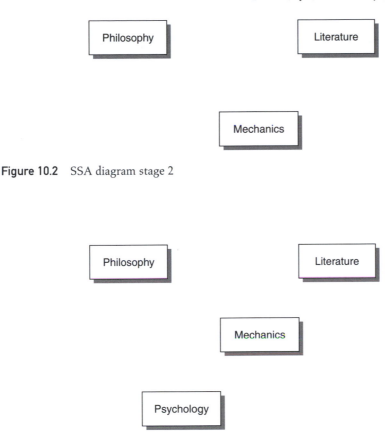

Figure 10.2   SSA diagram stage 2

Figure 10.3   SSA diagram stage 3

Now we add history (Figure 10.4), which is correlated with all the other variables and must be placed such that the relative strengths of correlation are shown in terms of relative distance in the spatial area.

The correlations between subjects are represented as locations in relative, diagrammatic, space. This portrayal reflects the relative correlational distances between the variables and meets what is called the 'monotone mapping condition'. Are there alternative configurations? Yes, as long as they meet the basic requirement that the relative distances reflect the relative indices of similarity (which in this case are correlations). If we had used a computer program these distances would have been determined exactly by mathematical processes.

The real world use of SSA, according to Guttman and Greenbaum (1998, p. 13), involves 'intelligence testing, attitude research, infant development, personal adjustment, human values, well-being, psychotherapy, organizational psychology, work values, environmental studies, animal behaviour, behavioural genetics,

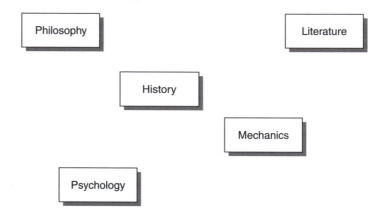

Figure 10.4 SSA diagram stage 4

nursing studies, suicidal behaviour, language development, curriculum development, distributive justice, crime scenes and offenders'. With such complex arrays of information it is often necessary to represent it in a variety of geometrical forms. Perhaps the most recognisable to social scientists is the circumplex, developed by Leary (1957) and utilised by Louis Guttman in the 1960s to develop ideas around SSA. The circumplex has since grown in size, application and complexity.

Guttman developed something he called a radex, which was a circumplex in three-dimensional form such that it resembled a cylinder that could then be further divided into levels. Some graphical representations resemble complex topographical maps, with closer relationships designated by the closeness of contour in the 'map'. Even these more complex graphical representations still rely on the same basic logic that those items that are more similar are grouped together in space and, in this sense, show their debt to factor analysis.

The original computer programs designed for performing SSA were developed by Guttman in the 1960s. Since then a variety of programs have become available which either are specific to facet theory and SSA or have the techniques as part of their repertoire. These include HUDAP, LiFA, SYSTAT, SAS and FSSA. HUDAP is the Hebrew University Data Analysis Program and is a suite of programs containing FSSA and WSSA1 for running SSAs. LiFA is a program developed by Liverpool University which is Windows based and easy to use, producing good-quality and easy-to-interpret diagrams. SYSTAT is a suite of different programs for statistical analysis that includes SSA. Like LiFA, it is Windows based and easy to use, generating colourful, three-dimensional diagrams. SYSTAT 11 is available through the SYSTAT website and you are able to download a trial copy for free. SAS incorporates an SSA component in a Windows environment; the outputs are perhaps not as slick as those generated by SYSTAT, but it is easy to use. DOS-Facets is a free, DOS-based program that is easy to use providing you are not scared of DOS and know a little coding. It requires that you download an .exe program, which many networked university systems do not allow.

EXAMPLES FROM PSYCHOLOGY, HEALTH AND BUSINESS

From psychology

In psychology, the accurate measurement of attitudes is often of paramount importance. Ben-Shalom and Horenczyk (2003) use facet theory and SSA to look at attitudes of different groups to assimilation (acculturation) into a society. Their study challenged previous research which suggested that when an immigrant group stayed in a host country for a period, its own ethnic or cultural identities gradually diminished in a somewhat linear fashion. They developed research questions using the mapping sentence technique and identified four primary facets based on previous research: separation, assimilation, integration and marginalisation. After using their questionnaires to interview groups of immigrants and non-immigrants, they analysed the results using the HUDAP program for SSA mentioned above. The results were presented as a radex diagram divided into the four facets, with the addition of two concentric circles to indicate the levels on which the concepts were significant (in this case, 'own' and 'expected', applying to views in acculturation). Within the radex are spread the identity issues under investigation; their relationships are clearly exhibited by their positions both with respect to each identity construct and with respect to where they fall within the four faceted areas. Their results challenge assumptions about immigrant identity by showing that it is constructed of a number of facets that have varying relationships. Overall, they demonstrate the usefulness of facet theory by showing a cogent example of how the technique is used in conjunction with SSA.

From health

The past 20 years has seen an increase in awareness around the nexus between physiological health and quality of life. Quality of life (QOL) is a construct that is defined and assessed differently by different organisations. For example, a local hospital may administer a survey to patients looking at QOL whereas the World Health Organization may administer a quite different instrument intended to assess the same 'QOL' but conceived differently.

Shye (1989) worked towards building a more compact conceptualisation of the key indicators for QOL using facet theory. The concept was explored by developing mapping sentences designed to assess the key indicators of QOL. The result was an SSA showing how closely the constituents of QOL are related and which ones seem to be the core elements. These core elements of the QOL survey were then applied to the study of QOL in an urban regeneration area.

Shye found that a combination of psychological, social, cultural and physical factors influenced QOL. Sometimes it was not simply about living in a 'bad neighbourhood' but how that neighbourhood was perceived – if, for example, the physical environment was in fact very poor but the person had strong social contacts characterised by being valued or having close friendships, then QOL might be higher than expected. What the study demonstrated is that there is an interaction between people and their environment, culture and social network and that these may be better predictors of QOL than measurements of apartment size or income.

From business

To develop business strategies it is important to know – or at least have an idea – what consumers want and how they are motivated. This example comes from a trade journal published by the Product Management Group (http://www.scientific-solutions.ch/tech/systat/resources/pdf/Consumer.pdf (accessed 1 June 2004)) and discusses some important tools marketers can use to gauge consumers. SSA was used to analyse consumer choice of beverages. A variety of different beverages from tea and coffee to milk and tomato juice which were rated on a scale of healthy, sweet, good, refreshing or simple tasting. People's preference for one category of drinks over another enabled marketers to tailor their products to taste.

FAQs

Is SSA different from factor analysis?

It isn't so different from factor analysis or principal components analysis, but the outputs are graphical. SSA has the flexibility to look at measures of similarity that may include correlations but can also use other measures.

Can SSA be used in isolation from facet theory?

It can, but together they form a comprehensive research package that provides a structured method to research that can help with development and analysis. The reverse may also be true: facet theory can be used to develop research questions and structures with the results analysed by some other method. But the loss would be in the elegance of the complete research package.

How is SSA different from multidimensional scaling?

They are the same essentially, though with MDS the relationships between concepts are precisely determined through an algorithm. SSA uses this technique in computer applications. Recall, however, that SSA can be determined in ways that are not necessarily mathematical (e.g. by a panel of experts).

SUMMARY

Facet theory is a total research package that allows the researcher to develop and implement a study systematically and provides a method for analysing the results through its adjunct smallest space analysis. Smallest space analysis is analogous to factor analysis but the output is visual. The premise of the visual representation of concepts in space is that those concepts which are more closely related will be closer together in geometric space. It does not, however, depend on statistical analysis and its proponents do not see this as problematic; they see this aspect as part of the flexibility of the approach. Smallest space diagrams, they note, can be organised by a panel of experts who may bring experience and qualitative information about relatedness which statistical procedures cannot account for. Some of the criticisms of facet theory centre around this flexibility. Holz-Ebeling (1990), for example, notes that facet theory is not a theory at all but a method that has as its goal a 'logical principle of thought' rather than a type of analysis or a type of theory. The proponents would probably smile at such a criticism and maybe even agree.

GLOSSARY

Domain the domain is composed of the focus set and the sense set and is the first part of constructing a mapping sentence. In the example mentioned above about apples, the focus set would have been the man whose name began with an 'R' with the sense set being what this man did with apples.

Mapping sentence the mapping sentence is composed of a focus set and a sense set together called the domain. The set of images, items, experiences, etc., to which the domain refers is called the range. Together the focus, sense and range are called the universe of observations. Essentially a device for research design, Shye (1998) defines the mapping sentence as '[a tool] for the formalization of the definitional framework for collecting data'.

Smallest space analysis a geometrical representation of similar concepts presented such that those that are more similar are closer together in space and those that are less similar are further away from one another. A key underlying theoretical notion here is that while some other methods treat concepts or variables as separate, measurable, entities, facet theory in general and smallest space analysis in particular treat these as part of some greater whole (called a concept universe). For example, intelligence might be treated as part of some array of concepts that might have as their constituents: positive attitude, affective management and empathy. Also, relationships are shown not as single abstract numbers but rather demonstrated by their 'mutual orientation of the regions in space' (Shye, 1998).

REFERENCES

Ben-Shalom, U. and Horenczyk, G. (2003). Accultural orientations: a facet theory approach on the bidimensional model. *Journal of Cross-Cultural Psychology*, 34, 176–188.

Guttman, R. and Greenbaum, C. (1998). Facet theory: its development and current status. *European Psychologist*, 3, 13–36.

Holz-Ebeling, F. (1990). Uneasiness with facet theory: time for a reappraisal. *Archiv für Psychologie* (Frankfurt am Main), 142, 265–293.

Leary, T. (1957). *The Interpersonal Theory of Psychiatry*. New York: Ronald.

Shye, S. (1989). The systemic life quality model: a basis for urban renewal evaluation. *Social Indicators Research*, 21, 343–378.

Shye, S. (1998). Modern facet theory: content design and measurement in behavioral research. *European Journal of Psychological Assessment*, 14, 160–171.

Shye, S., Elizur, D. and Hoffman, M. (1994). *Introduction to Facet Theory: Content Designs and Intrinsic Data Analysis in Behavioral Research*. London: Sage.

Young, F. and Hamer, R. (1987). *Multidimensional Scaling: History, Theory and Applications*. New York: Erlbaum.

FURTHER READING

Borg, I. and Shye, S. (1995). *Facet Theory: Form and Content*. Thousand Oaks, CA: Sage.

Canter, D. (1985). *Facet Theory: Approaches to Social Research*. New York: Springer.

Guttman, L. (1971). Measurement as structural theory. *Psychometrika*, 36, 329–347.

11

Survival or Failure Analysis

WHAT SURVIVAL/FAILURE ANALYSIS IS

The terms survival or failure analysis are used interchangeably to refer to the same procedure. They reflect the fields for which the technique was developed. On the one hand, medical practitioners and epidemiologists use it to determine the rate or time taken for an event to occur. On the other, in industrial development and testing the influence of stress or exposure on the time taken for equipment or components to fail is examined. In either case the event which the researcher is waiting to happen needs to be fixed and objectively measurable, and can only occur once in the study period. The analysis can compare different groups (of people or components) and can also be used to determine the effects of a number of predictors on survival time. For simplicity, this chapter will refer to cases as participants although they could be components in machinery.

WHEN DO YOU NEED SURVIVAL ANALYSIS?

The research questions addressed by survival analysis are concerned with the time taken for an event, such as dying or becoming ill, to happen from the point in time at which observations begin. The technique assumes that the factors which influenced survival at the start of the study are present throughout the time period observed without additional factors (uncontrolled by the researcher) being introduced. The definitions of both the entry and end (or 'exit') point for participants should remain consistent throughout the study. It is good research practice for these to be objectively defined.

ISSUES IN DESIGNING RESEARCH FOR SURVIVAL ANALYSIS

It is assumed that the sample used in any study is randomly selected. In practice a truly random sample is difficult to achieve, so it is important to ensure that the sample included in any survival analysis study is representative of the population from which participants have been drawn. The generalisability of results is restricted if the sample is not representative, but in practice the sample often consists of those who are willing to take part. Therefore, general demographic and other relevant information should be reported to demonstrate the degree to which the sample is representative of the population from which participants are drawn.

One feature of survival analysis is that it has a method of taking into account 'missing' end observations, known as censored data. For example, suppose a researcher is following the effects of a new antipsychotic medication on patients with schizophrenia over a period of one year in order to determine whether it significantly increases the time they spend out of hospital. Examples of censored data would be: (1) some participants may not return to hospital until after the one year follow-up period, so their hospitalisation will be an unobserved event (this is an example of fixed-right censoring); (2) some participants will be lost and simply not report to be followed up and so they will become missing data (this is random-right censoring); (3) some participants may have come out of hospital prior to the study starting and would not return to hospital regardless of the treatment which they received (this is left-censoring).

Fixed-right censoring is always fixed since it is dictated by the period of follow-up set by the researcher; some participants will reach the end event after the follow-up has been closed. Random-right censoring is the equivalent of missing data points in other statistical methods. This type of censoring is random since it occurs owing to events outside the researcher's control. Right-censored observations, either fixed or random, occur with greater frequency than left-censored observations. Random censoring is thought to be independent of the survival time. However, there are occasions where it may not be: for example, someone whose illness is very severe may not be able to attend the project's follow-up appointments. The censored cases are not supposed to differ from those who were observed throughout the study. If they do, it indicates a potential confound in the study since the missing data points are non-random.

If participants leave the study for reasons unrelated to the research question, an appropriate method of coding these individuals needs to be developed. For example, if the study is concerned with the survival rates in a group of cardio-vascular patients and a number die from a cause unrelated to their heart condition, would these individuals be classified as dead (i.e. reaching the end point in the study) or as censored observations? Either method is appropriate as long as it is used consistently and made explicit in the description of the analysis used.

WHAT KINDS OF DATA ARE NEEDED?

The data in survival analysis are the number of participants and the time taken for a defined event to occur, for example in psychiatry, the time taken to remission or to reoccurrence of a depressive episode. The end point of the survival data should be an event which occurs only once: it is not possible to use survival analysis to study events which occur more than once over time. (In order to make the description in this chapter generalisable to any example, the term 'end point' will be used to denote the defined exit from the study. It could be death, hospital admission, remission, etc.) The survival times in any sample are generally not going to approximate to a normal distribution. Therefore, survival analysis is classified as an essentially non-parametric technique. Survival analysis is able to handle continuous covariates, compare groups of participants and determine what factors most effectively predict survival time.

BASIC OUTLINE AND TYPES OF SURVIVAL ANALYSIS

Life tables

Life tables are used to describe the patterns of mortality over various time points. In a life table, the total sample is referred to as the radix. The time intervals may be yearly, but they can be any appropriate interval. The production and inter-pretation of a general population life table has three assumptions: (1) the number of births remains constant from year to year; (2) after 4 years of age the number of deaths are normally distributed; and (3) the number of deaths is offset by the number of births, and no large-scale immigration or emigration takes place, that is the population size remains relatively constant. If these three assumptions are met, the population is said to be stationary. A truly stationary population does not exist in the world today, but if the three assumptions are not violated too grossly then the use of life tables is taken to be valid.

Life tables are not produced by following up individuals from birth to death. They can be considered a snapshot of mortality in a particular country at a moment in time. They give both epidemiologists and sociologists useful informa-tion about the inferred state of conditions of living and life expectation over time.

As an example, Kalèdienè and Petrauskienè (2004) were interested in the effects health developments had had on life and health expectancy in people in Lithuania. They produced life tables for the years 1997 and 2001 and compared expected years of healthy life at birth in males and females for both years. Healthy life expectancy in females increased from 52.6 to 55.3 years between 1997 and 2001; for males, it increased from 52.7 to 53.7 years. The authors concluded that health developments had had some positive impact on the health expectancy of people living in Lithuania. However, it seemed that although women were living longer they experienced longer periods of poor health. The use of health expectancy rather than just life expectancy highlighted that there were still improvements to be made in the health of people in Lithuania especially after the age of 30.

Life tables are also produced for the mortality rate of individuals with specific illnesses such as heart disease or cancer. Comparison of the hazard functions of different groups can be used to highlight the age ranges which are most at risk of the illness and therefore identify groups which need to be targeted for interventions. Comparison across different years may reflect improvements in treatment for illnesses. Louhimo et al. (2004), for example, display percentage survival time to two years follow-up for 146 individuals with gastric cancer and the correlations with a number of clinicopathological variables. The authors suggest that as well as serum tumour markers being useful in determining prognosis in gastric cancer, additional clinical variables such as location and tumour size are also informative for clinicians' expectations of their patients' survival rate two years after diagnosis.

Survival curve

A survival curve represents the probability of surviving to the end point as a function of time. An example is shown in Figure 11.1. The area under the curve approximates to the value for expectation of life and the slope of the curve is the intensity of mortality. The median survival time can be found by finding the point where 50% of the participants have reached the defined end point. (From the vertical axis at the point corresponding to 50% survival, draw a horizontal to the curve; then draw a vertical from the point of intersection down to the time axis. This gives the median survival time.)

There are two approaches to computing survival curves from life tables: the actuarial method and the Kaplan–Meier or product-limited method. Using the actuarial method, the time axis is divided into equal intervals, such as months or years, and survival is calculated at each interval by dividing the number surviving at each time period by the original number of participants.

An alternative is to use the Kaplan–Meier or product-limit method of calculating the survival function. Although it is laborious to calculate, the principle behind it is simple. Each time the defined time interval has passed, the number surviving to the end of that period is calculated as a proportion of the number who had survived to the start of that period. The proportion for any one time period is multiplied by the proportions of all preceding time periods. If there are no censored data points, the actuarial and Kaplan–Meier method produce the same results, but when there are many censored points the Kaplan–Meier is the most appropriate method because the censored individuals are taken into account. The Kaplan–Meier method has the advantage over the actuarial method that it can produce a mean value of survival time for comparing groups of participants.

The Kaplan–Meier curve is particularly useful in medical science. Bollschweiler (2003) discusses its application to cancer research, arguing that the consideration

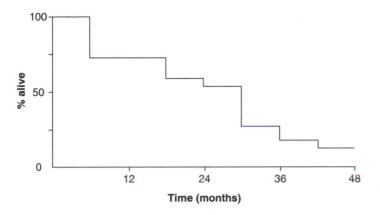

Figure 11.1   Example of a survival curve

of censored data points is a strength of the Kaplan–Meier method but noting that certain recommendations should be followed. For example, the right side of survival curves, where many patients have been censored, becomes increasingly uncertain due to small sample size; the cut-off point should be defined as the point where there are only, say, 10–20% of the original sample size left in the study. Bollschweiler states that although many studies give the mean follow-up time, this is inappropriate since the survival data is highly skewed; showing the median follow-up time and displaying the number of patients still event-free at each time point would be more useful statistics to present. Additionally, confidence intervals should be displayed to demonstrate the increasing variation in the data with decreasing sample sizes as you move to the right of the curve. Information about participants who do not complete the study is often omitted from reports of patient survival; a measure of completeness such as the ratio of total observed person-time to potential person-time should be reported and can be used to identify groups with particularly poor follow-up.

Hlatky et al. (2002) describe the use of the Kaplan–Meier curve to model the economic assessment of a 10-year follow-up study of patients who had received coronary bypass surgery or coronary angioplasty. The use of the Kaplan–Meier curve appealed to these authors since it allowed for censored data points to be considered by the analysis. They calculated the treatment costs, controlling for both inflation and interest rates over the study period, and produced separate curves for those who received bypass surgery and those who received coronary angioplasty, with a follow-up of up to eight years. The cumulative cost curves for both groups of patients show a steady rise over the years of follow-up. Initially the costs of the angioplasty were 35% lower than for bypass, but by the end of the follow-up the difference between the two procedures was only 4% (with angioplasty remaining slightly cheaper). The authors also used the area underneath the Kaplan–Meier curve and the cost of both treatments to consider the cost-effectiveness of the two treatments in terms of years survived over an eight-year follow-up. Initially, the bypass surgery does badly since it is a more expensive treatment. But over the years of follow-up it becomes much more cost effective since it has a better survival outcome (even though the difference between the interventions was only 3% for survival rate) and also displays reducing cumulative costs.

Hazard function

The inverse of the survival curve is the hazard function or curve which reflects the risk of death. The cumulative hazard function is the number of deaths occurring over a time period and in essence is just an alternative method of displaying the hazards over time.

As with other types of survival analysis, hazard functions are primarily used in a health care setting. In New Zealand in 2001, health reforms were introduced which implemented a maximum waiting time for all general surgery procedures. MacCormick and Parry (2003) report the hazard functions for patients waiting for elective surgery. The hazard functions reflected the probability that someone had not had the operation they were waiting for. At 180 days the hazard function was largest for those with malignancy and smallest for hernias. At 360 days the hazard function for malignancy was zero, smallest for hernias and largest for cholelithiasis. At 540 days the hazard functions were zero for all disease groups except anorectal disease. MacCormick and Parry concluded that the six-month waiting cut-off did not work for all disease groups: 'if a single threshold were required by funders, a more suitable cut-off could be 1 year, as determined from the survival curves' (p. 927).

Cox's proportional model

Cox's proportional or hazard model is a form of regression model applicable to survival data because it does not assume the dependent variable is normally distributed and it can deal with censored data. It offers the opportunity to investigate more fully factors which influence survival time and to compare two groups which differ in some way (such as comparing time in remission for two groups of cancer patients who could have received different treatments). It is primarily used in health and medical sciences.

As an example, there are reported differences in the rates of mortality for alcohol-related deaths by socio-economic group: those from lower socio-economic groups are more likely to die from alcohol-related illnesses. Mäkelä et al. (2003) investigated, using Finnish data, whether there is just a lower survival rate in lower socio-economic groups in general rather than it being specifically related to alcohol consumption. They examined the mortality rates in males and females over 15 years of age who had had a hospital discharge for an alcohol-related illness. Participants, followed up from 1991 to 1995, were divided into three groups according to their main diagnosis (alcoholic disease of the liver or pancreas; alcohol dependent, alcohol psychoses and 'other'; intoxication), and divided into age groups: 15–44, 45–59, 60 + years. For the alcohol-dependent category there was an interaction between age and socio-economic status: younger males who were upper white-collar workers had a higher mortality rate. The authors used Cox's proportional model to produce hazard ratios for the different alcohol diagnoses groups and age groups, and controlled for gender, hospital, length of stay in hospital and cause of admittance to hospital. The authors concluded that they had found a reversal of the previous findings for a socio-economic gradient in deaths related to alcohol use. However, their results suggested that differences in rates of death from alcohol-related illness could not be explained by differences in hospital stay, type of disease or type of hospital, since these were controlled for in their model. They do acknowledge that those in the higher socio-economic groups may delay seeking treatment and thus present with more severe illness which is more likely to lead to death.

EXAMPLES OF SURVIVAL ANALYSIS

From health

'Anticipation' is a phenomenon reported in diseases such as schizophrenia and refers to the age of onset decreasing and/or severity increasing with successive generations within the same family suffering from the disease. Stompe et al. (2000) reported the results from a study of 380 patients with schizophrenia from Austria. Information from the patients' medical notes was used in two survival analysis methods, Cox's and Kaplan–Meier, to determine which factors influenced the onset of schizophrenia. The authors recorded data on a range of variables including year of birth, age at onset, first- and second-degree relatives afflicted with schizophrenia, education of patient, age of parents, occupation of parents and place of residence. From Cox's analysis, onset of disease was found to be influenced by family history (with sporadic cases having an onset two years later than those with family history), and urbanicity: those who lived in urban regions displayed psychotic symptoms a year earlier. Additionally, year of birth had a significant effect on age of onset. To examine this relationship further, the authors performed the Kaplan–Meier method, separating the sample into three birth cohorts: 1935–1944, 1945–1954, 1955–1964. The study demonstrated that the effect of birth cohort was explained by both sporadic and familial cases of schizophrenia having earlier onset as the years passed.

To explain the decreasing age of onset by cohort effect, the authors concluded that decrease in infant mortality might have led to more 'at risk' children surviving to the age of onset of schizophrenia where previously childhood illnesses would have led to their early demise. Additionally, the increase in the pace of life in Austria may be indicative of other factors, such as social stressors, which could decrease the age of onset of schizophrenia in those at risk of developing it. The results that familial cases of schizophrenia had an onset which was two years earlier than their sporadic counterparts can be explained by family environment rather than genetic influences. Additionally, urbanicity was thought to be indicative of other risk factors such as lack of social support networks and life stresses.

From industrial health

An example of the use of Cox's proportional model in the occupational arena is that of Kraut et al. (2004). Their paper examines mortality in a group of industrial workers and the role which religious beliefs may play. Religious beliefs have been reported to have a protective effect against death in many groups of people and the ability (or rather capability) to attend church does not fully explain this relationship. The sample consisted of 3638 Jewish Israeli males who were followed up over a 12-year period. Overall the religious group of men did not have lower mortality rates than the other employees. In employees who were younger than 55 years, religiousness was associated with lower mortality. Among employees who were 55 years or older, however, religiousness was associated with higher mortality, and this remained significant after controlling for socio-economic status and workplace conditions. The authors suggest that the lack of protection from religiousness in those aged 55 and over may be mediated by variables other than those investigated in their study, such as lack of social integration in the workplace.

FAQs

Why go to the trouble of using survival analysis when you could just compare mean survival time between groups?

Simply comparing the mean survival time of two groups omits much of the information which survival analysis can provide. The shape of the survival curve over time can give you answers to questions such as 'are people reaching the end point quickly, with a few people surviving beyond the follow-up point?' or 'are people reaching the end point a long time after entering the study with many participants reaching the end point at the same time?' These questions would not be answered by comparing mean survival times. Also, comparing only the mean survival times would give no consideration to censored data points and when they occur.

What happens if censored data is not normally distributed?

This usually indicates that there are uncharacterised reasons why these individuals have left the study or become lost at follow-up. A questionnaire can be sent to those who have left the study to enquire about the reasons for their leaving. (However, there is a fine line between investigative curiosity and hounding participants who have left your study!)

SUMMARY

Survival analysis concerns the time taken for an event to happen. The data consists of the number of participants and the time taken for the defined event to occur. Missing end observations, known as censored data, are of different types: fixed-right censoring, random-right censoring and left-censoring.

A survival curve represents the probability of surviving to the end point as a function of time, and its inverse is the hazard curve. Cox's proportional or hazard model is a form of regression model applicable to survival data, primarily used in health and medical sciences.

GLOSSARY

Censored data   an event which occurs unobserved by the researcher.

Fixed-right censoring   when the end event occurs after the set period of time of experimental observation or follow-up.

Hazard curve or function   the graphical depiction of the rate of death over time for a sample.

Left-censoring   when the end event occurs before the start of the observation for the study.

Life table   a table displaying the number of people to die over a period of time.

Radix   the total sample represented in a life table.

Random-right censoring   when the participant leaves the study before the follow-up period has been completed and before the end event has occurred.

Stationary population   when the size of the population remains relatively stable over time.

Survival curve or function   the graphical depiction of the rate of survival over time for a sample.

REFERENCES

Bollschweiler, E. (2003). Benefits and limitations of Kaplan–Meier calculations of survival chance in cancer surgery. *Langenbecks Archives of Surgery*, 388, 239–244.

Hlatky, M.A., Boothroyd, D.B. and Johnstone, I.M. (2002). Economic evaluation in long-term clinical trials. *Statistics in Medicine*, 21, 2879–2888.

Kalédiené, R. and Petrauskiené, J. (2004). Healthy life expectancy – an important indicator for health policy development in Lithuania. *Medicina (Kaunas)*, 40, 582–588.

Kraut, A., Melamed, S., Gofer, D. and Froom, P. (2004). Association of self reported religiosity and mortality in industrial employees: the CORDIS study. *Social Science and Medicine*, 58, 595–602.

Louhimo, J., Kokkola, A., Alfthan, H., Stenman, U. and Haglund, C. (2004). Preoperative hCGβ and CA 72-4 are prognostic factors in gastric cancer. *International Journal of Cancer*, 111, 929–933.

MacCormick, A.D. and Parry, B.R. (2003). Waiting time thresholds: are they appropriate? *Australian and New Zealand Journal of Surgery*, 73, 926–928.

Mäkelä, P., Keskimäki, I.T. and Koskinen, S. (2003). What underlies the high alcohol related mortality of the disadvantaged: high morbidity or poor survival? *Journal of Epidemiology and Community Health*, 57, 981–986.

Stompe, T., Ortwein-Swoboda, G., Strobl, R. and Friedmann, A. (2000). The age of onset of schizophrenia and the theory of anticipation. *Psychiatry Research*, 93 (2), 125–134.

FURTHER READING

Cole, S.R. and Hernan, M.A. (2004). Adjusted survival curves with inverse probability weights. *Computer Methods and Programs for Biomedicine*, 75 (1), 45–49.

Collett, D. (2003). *Modelling Survival Data in Medical Research*. London: Chapman and Hall/CRC Press.

Harrell, F. (2001). *Regression Modeling Strategies: with Applications to Linear Models, Logistic Regression, and Survival Analysis*. New York: Springer.

Hosmer, D.W. (1999). *Applied Survival Analysis: Regression Modeling of Time to Event Data*. New York: Wiley.

Hougaard, P. (2000). *Analysis of Multivariate Survival Data*. New York: Springer.

Lee, E.T. (2003). *Statistical Methods for Survival Data Analysis*. New York: Wiley.

Marubini, E. and Grazia Valsecchi, M. (1995). *Analysing Survival Data from Clinical Trials and Observation Studies*. Chichester: Wiley.

Mathew, A., Pandey, M. and Murthy, N.S. (1999). Survival analysis: caveats and pitfalls. *European Journal of Surgical Oncology*, 25, 321–329.

Selvin, S. (1996). *Statistical Analysis of Epidemiology Data* (2nd edn). New York: Oxford University Press.

Troxel, A.B. (2002). Techniques for incorporating longitudinal measurements into analyses of survival data from clinical trials. *Statistical Methods in Medical Research*, 11 (3), 237–245.

INTERNET SOURCES

www.orthoteers.co.uk

http://bmj.bmjjournals.com/collections/statsbk/12.shtml

http://www.orthoteers.co.uk/Nrujp~ij33lm/Orthstatssurvival.htm

12

Repertory Grids

WHAT REPERTORY GRIDS ARE

Repertory grids are a tool for getting respondents to reveal the constructs they use in interpreting (construing) the world around them. Developed in the context of personality theory and psychotherapy or counselling, repertory tools have been used to investigate the differences between people and the changes which occur when people undergo transitions such as counselling or moving into employment.

INTRODUCTION TO REPERTORY GRIDS

Many of the methods used by social scientists to obtain data involve people reporting about themselves – what they believe, how they feel, their attitude to some event or concept. The most common way in which these feelings or attitudes are assessed is by some form of questionnaire, and in very many instances the alternative answers are provided – the respondents might be asked to select between 'yes' and 'no' or asked to indicate their feeling by using some kind of rating scale such as indicating how much they agree with a statement using a scale running from 'strongly agree' to 'strongly disagree'. One drawback to these types of questions is that they constrain the respondent – only the alternatives provided are available, and the questions have been written by someone else and may not reflect the way the respondent thinks about things. Everyone has their own way of looking at the world, resulting from their own experience and what they have been told, and giving a questionnaire may not allow one to discover what that way is or how it is structured.

The notion that every individual has their own way of looking at the world, their own unique structure of concepts they use to interpret events, is the foundation of Kelly's personal construct theory which was described in *The Psychology of*

Personal Constructs in 1955. As the name implies, this theory proposed that everyone has their own personal set of concepts or constructs and to understand someone's view of an area one needs to be aware of their constructs and how these constructs are structured. (Burr and Butt (1992)) emphasise that concepts and constructs are not the same things. They argue that 'concept' is a term from logic and is a kind of category into which things are put on the basis of some common factor or classification system. But 'we have "constructs" in the same way that we have questions and it makes more sense to talk about construing as something we do. Construing is a process …. Construing is how we use concepts' (p. 14). But one cannot simply ask people what constructs they apply and how they are related to each other, because the system is so ingrained in the person that it is not open to simple introspection. One needs a technique which will reveal the constructs and their structure, both to the person and to the person applying the technique.

Kelly developed a method for doing this, and this repertory grid procedure has become a widespread method for probing a person's construct structure. (There are in fact a number of variants so it might be better to refer to repertory grid procedures, but we shall describe the basic method and point out some of the variations as we go along.)

There are two basic components of a repertory grid: elements and constructs. One starts with elements: entities (things, people or events) pertinent to that part of the person's construct system which one is investigating. For example, if you were examining someone's constructs about themselves then the elements might include 'me as I am', 'me as I would like to be', 'my mother', 'my father', 'the brother or sister I like most', 'someone I love'. If you were examining someone's constructs concerned with jobs and work, the elements might be 'a job I would like to do', 'my current job', 'a job I would not like', 'my ideal job', 'a well-paid job', 'a socially valuable job'. The person is asked to give particular examples which fit these general descriptors and use them in the next stage of the procedure.

The second stage involves presenting three particular elements (a triad) and asking the respondent to indicate which two go together and which is the odd one out, and then to say what is the feature underlying this grouping – what it is that the two which go together have which the odd one out does not have. The feature which the respondent provides is the emergent pole of the construct. It is usual to ask the respondent to say what is the other end of the emergent pole of the construct; so if it is said that two elements go together and differ from the third one because the two are 'polite', the respondent is asked to say what is the feature of the odd element which means it is not seen as 'polite'. The opposite end of the construct, known as the contrast pole, may be the normal opposite, 'impolite' in this example. But often this is not the case: the two may be 'polite' but the third may be described as 'aggressive' or 'noisy' or some other feature. The intention is to get respondents to state their own constructs, defined as they use them.

Triads of different elements are presented a number of times, and a different construct obtained each time. The responses are then analysed to show how the constructs and the elements are related to each other.

Examples of a response form and the type of output which can be obtained are shown in Figure 12.1 and Figure 12.2; the construct system concerned with jobs was being investigated. Here, the respondent provided the constructs 'mainly uses brains–not using brains', 'indoor–outdoor', 'useful–not very useful', 'very skilful–less skilful' and 'having an unreliable career–having a reliable career'. As is shown in Figure 12.2, one can ask the respondent to rate each element on each of the constructs – in this example, a five-point scale was used with 5 representing a high level of the emergent pole shown in the right-hand column of the figure and 1 representing a high level on the opposite end of the construct, the contrast pole. But it is not necessary to have ratings: one can ask the respondent simply to indicate which elements have the emergent pole feature and which do not, in which case one obtains a dichotomous grid. Another alternative is to have the respondent rank the elements on the construct; in the example shown in Figure 12.2 one would ask the respondent to indicate which element was highest on 'mainly uses brains', which came second on that construct and so on.

You, the reader, may not agree that the attributes shown in Figure 12.2 are the important features of a job and may not agree with the ratings shown in Figure 12.2, where for example it can be seen that the respondent indicates that he or she believes a steeplejack does not use brains very much and is not very useful either. But that is one of the points of the repertory grid procedure – to have respondents reveal their constructs and how they place the elements on those constructs.

The repertory grid technique has become increasingly popular for individual counselling and is a useful way of helping the development of self-insight. As the results are personal to the individual respondent, it cannot readily be used for groups of people although attempts to do so have been made; some examples are described below.

WHEN DO YOU NEED REPERTORY GRID ANALYSIS?

Repertory grids are used to reveal an individual's conceptual structure, to uncover how the person groups the elements, which constructs they use and how the constructs are related to each other. One application is in counselling, where one might administer grids before and after the counselling process to see what changes have taken place (e.g. Leach et al., 2001). Repertory grids have also been applied in industrial contexts for evaluating training and identifying management potential. (An introduction to the applications of repertory grids in business is available from Enquire Within at www.EnquireWithin.co.nz (retrieved 23 August 2004).)

1 Write the name of a job which fits each description. Use a different job for each one, and write the name under each description. For example, if you thought 'a well-paid job' described the job of a bus driver, you would write 'bus driver' under that phrase on the dotted line.

-Cn	A	B	C	D	E	F	Cn
	a job I would like to do	my current job	a job I would not like	my ideal job	a well-paid job	a socially valuable job	

1
2
3
4
5

2 Now think about the jobs you have written in under A, B and C. Which two go together, and which is the odd one out? Put a cross on the first line under the odd one out, and a tick under the two that go together.

3 Now give a word or phrase which describes how the two jobs that 'go together' differ from the odd one out. Write it on the first line in the column on the right headed Cn.

4 Give a word or phrase which describes how the odd one differs from the two which you have said go together. Write it on the first line in the column on the left headed -Cn.

5 <u>Either</u> Now put a tick on the first line under every one of the jobs which has the feature you have written in the CN column and a cross under every one of the jobs which does not have that feature.
   <u>Or</u> Give a score on a scale from 1 to 5 for each of the jobs on the attribute you gave at step 3 and put the scores under each job on the first line.

6 Now think about the jobs you have written in under B, D and E. Which two go together, and which is the odd one out? Put a cross on the second line under the odd one out, and a tick under the two that go together.

7 Now give a word or phrase which describes how the two jobs that 'go together' differ from the odd one out. Write it on the second line in the column on the right headed Cn.

8 Give a word or phrase which describes how the odd one differs from the two which you have said go together. Write it on the second line in the column on the left headed -Cn.

9 <u>Either</u> Now put a tick on the second line under every one of the jobs which has the feature you have written in the Cn column and a cross under every one of the jobs which does not have that feature.
   <u>Or</u> Give a score on a scale from 1 to 5 for each of the jobs on the attribute you gave at step 7 and put the scores under each job on the second line.

10 Repeat the procedure three more times, using the jobs you have written in under B, E and F; then the jobs you have written in under A, D and F and finally the jobs you have written in under B, C, E. Use a separate line for each set of responses so you end up with either ticks and crosses or numbers on each line and the relevant words in columns Cn and -Cn.

When completed, a grid such as this can be analysed in two directions. First, the way the constructs (the entries in the column headed Cn) are used and how they are related to each other can be studied to reveal the respondent's personal construct system. Secondly, the relationship between the elements can be studied, and their position in the construct structure (construct space) can reveal the similarities and differences between the way they are regarded by the respondent.

Figure 12.1 Repertory grid technique

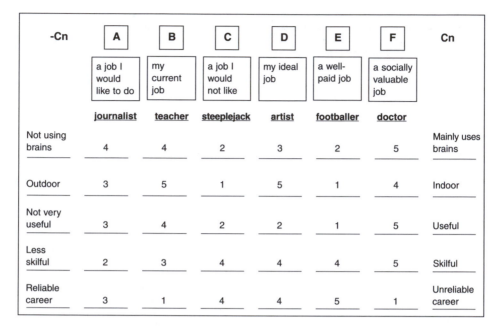

-Cn	A	B	C	D	E	F	Cn
	a job I would like to do	my current job	a job I would not like	my ideal job	a well-paid job	a socially valuable job	
	journalist	teacher	steeplejack	artist	footballer	doctor	
Not using brains	4	4	2	3	2	5	Mainly uses brains
Outdoor	3	5	1	5	1	4	Indoor
Not very useful	3	4	2	2	1	5	Useful
Less skilful	2	3	4	4	4	5	Skilful
Reliable career	3	1	4	4	5	1	Unreliable career

Figure 12.2 Example of completed repertory grid

The development of grids was in the context of studying individuals, and not really intended to be aggregated across a number of individuals. But attempts have been made to compare sets of individuals in terms of their use of constructs. There are obvious problems if one has grids from a number of people and the elements and the constructs differ in every grid. One frequently used compromise has been to provide at least some of the constructs for the respondent. If one provides both the elements and the constructs, the technique resembles a conventional rating task (and is similar to the semantic differential procedure): it becomes rather far removed from the original ideas which spawned it. Some ways to analyse sets of grids are described below.

HOW YOU DO REPERTORY GRID ANALYSIS

There are two main approaches to analysing grids. The first one reflects the fact that grids are usually used on an individual basis to explore the construct system of a single person, although this may involve studying the changes in the responses given as the person passes through some transition process. Individual grids are examined to see how the constructs are related to each other and how the elements are related. If comparing a person's responses at different times, one may examine the grids obtained on the two occasions and use clinical interpretation of the changes between the two grids.

The second approach uses repertory grid methodology to compare groups of people, and this poses a problem of how to obtain some form of group or aggregate data when one has used an instrument not really designed for the purpose.

ANALYSING INDIVIDUAL GRIDS

There are alternative ways of analysing individual grids. Fransella et al. (2004) point out how, if one has obtained ratings of each element on each construct, simple statistics such as the mean and standard deviation for each construct can provide useful information. For example, they can show if one construct is lopsided, with most of the elements being rated high (or low), and whether the elements are more widely dispersed on some constructs than others. Leach et al. (2001) describe a number of methods for analysing individual grids, using an example of a grid in which nine elements had been rated on each of 14 constructs, 11 of which had been provided and 3 had been elicited using the triarchic procedure described above. They describe five forms of analysis, all of which can be done using a computer although some can be done manually. Four of the five forms of analysis concern individual grids and can be applied to ratings, dichotomous grids or rankings. Leach et al. point out that the different forms of analysis make different assumptions, and state 'it helps to do more than one analysis at a time … partly to notice different patterns emphasized by the different methods' (p. 229), which indicates that there is no single right way of performing the analysis.

The first form of analysis involves the clinical interpretation of the grid and this can be assisted if it is rearranged so that elements with similar data are placed adjacent to each other. (A computer program such as FOCUS can do this rather laborious task.)

An initial question concerns how far the elements are similar or dissimilar. The similarity between elements can be expressed using a Euclidean distance measure: one takes two elements and on each of the constructs squares the difference between the ratings, then sums these squares and divides by a constant such as the number of constructs. In Figure 12.2, comparing elements A and B the differences on the five constructs are $0, -2, -1, -1, 2$, so the squares are 0, 4, 1, 1 and 4 and the sum of these is 10. Dividing this by the number of constructs gives a value of 2. (If the differences are summed without being squared, giving a value of -2, one is using a city-block measure of distance.) Leach et al. observe that one should not use conventional correlation coefficients to assess the similarity between elements. (The reason is that one may want to reverse the scoring on a construct so that a high figure always denotes a desirable or positive judgement; if one does this, the size of the correlation will alter because the variance of the figures will be changed. Leach et al. note that some computer programs for grid analysis ignore this and can provide potentially misleading analyses.)

However, if one wishes to examine how far constructs (as opposed to elements) are related then a conventional correlation may be appropriate. If the grid is completed using ratings, a Pearson correlation coefficient is used; for rankings, one uses the Spearman correlation; and if the grid contains dichotomous data the phi-coefficient is appropriate. Fransella et al. (2004) note that a correlation coefficient is symmetrical: the correlation between a and b is the same as the correlation between b and a. But the relationships between constructs may be asymmetrical: the relationship between construct a and construct b might not be the same as the relationship between b and a. This is because constructs might be in superordinate/subordinate relationships: the construct 'involves demanding work' may imply 'is well paid', but 'is well paid' may not imply 'involves demanding work'. The authors point out that there are asymmetric measures of association one can use, including Somers' d if one has ratings or rankings in the grid. (The formula for Somers' d and an example of its calculation is provided by Blaikie, 2003.)

The structure of the relationship between elements or between constructs can be analysed using principal components analysis, a form of factor analysis, or multidimensional scaling. Both of these can provide plots of elements or constructs on a two-dimensional surface. Alternatively, one can use hierarchical cluster analysis to obtain a tree-like structure showing how the elements or constructs form clusters. All these forms of analysis can be obtained using standard statistical packages such as SPSS or SYSTAT.

Bell (1997) describes how SPSS can be used to analyse grids. It is relatively straightforward to obtain simple statistics on a grid, such as the mean for each element across constructs (and the converse: the mean for each construct across elements), and the distance between the ratings for one element and another. One can use principal components analysis or factor analysis to examine the correlations between constructs. Clustering analysis and multidimensional scaling can be used to study the relationships between the elements or between the constructs. (If you are using SPSS, these require rather complex procedures and some require the user to ensure the program uses absolute values of correlations or squared correlation values to remove negatives.)

An example of the results of using SPSS to perform a principal components analysis of the five constructs of the grid shown in Figure 12.2 is shown in Figure 12.3. The output shows that two components were extracted, one accounting for 67.9% of the variance the second accounting for 20.4%. Constructs C1 (mainly uses brains), C3 (useful) and C5 (having an unreliable career) load on the first component over 0.96. Construct C5's loading is negative, so one may wish to reverse this construct by changing the rating of 1 to 5, the rating of 2 to 4, the rating of 4 to 2 and the rating of 5 to 1. (This would mean that a rating of

```
FACTOR
    /VARIABLES c1 c2 c3 c4 c5 /MISSING LISTWISE /ANALYSIS c1 c2 c3 c4 c5
    /PRINT INITIAL EXTRACTION
    /CRITERIA MINEIGEN(1) ITERATE(25)
    /EXTRACTION PC
    /ROTATION NOROTATE
    /METHOD=CORRELATION.
```

Communalities

	Initial	Extraction
C1	1.000	.924
C2	1.000	.630
C3	1.000	.946
C4	1.000	.988
C5	1.000	.927

Extraction Method: Principal Component Analysis.

Total Variance Explained

Component	Initial Eigenvalues			Extraction Sums of Squared Loadings		
	Total	% of Variance	Cumulative %	Total	% of Variance	Cumulative %
1	3.393	67.856	67.856	3.393	67.856	67.856
2	1.022	20.440	88.296	1.022	20.440	88.296
3	.470	9.400	97.695			
4	.110	2.198	99.893			
5	.005	.107	100.000			

Extraction Method: Principal Component Analysis.

Component Matrix(a)

	Component	
	1	2
C1	.960	−.039
C2	.783	−.129
C3	.965	.122
C4	−.009	.994
C5	−.963	−.030

Extraction Method: Principal Component Analysis.

a 2 components extracted.

Figure 12.3 Output from principal components analysis of the grid responses shown in Figure 12.2

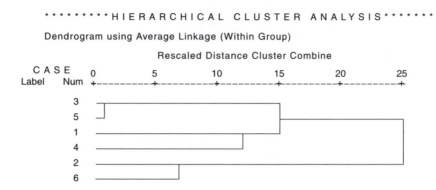

Figure 12.4 Dendrogram showing the clustering of the elements

1 would mean 'having a reliable career' and a rating of 5 would mean 'having an unreliable career', the opposite of the present meanings. If one does this, the loadings on the components are identical except that for C5 the loading on the first component becomes positive rather than negative.) C2 (indoor) loads on the first component 0.78 and C4 (very skilful) loads on it not at all but does load highly on the second component (0.994).

Figure 12.4 illustrates the SPSS output following hierarchical cluster analysis on the same grid. It shows a tree-like structure, known as a dendrogram, in which the elements form clusters according to their proximity. Elements 3 (a job I would not like) and 5 (a well-paid job) form the first, closest cluster. Elements 2 (my current job) and 6 (a socially valuable job) form the next cluster and elements 1 (a job I would like) and 4 (my ideal job) form the third one. The second and third clusters then join to make up the higher order cluster before that one joins with the first cluster to form the final overall cluster. (A similar form of analysis can be applied to constructs, using the absolute values of the correlations between them to order the sequence in which the constructs join clusters.)

Elements and constructs can be represented jointly if one uses a dedicated grid analysis program such as FOCUS or a technique such as biplot analysis which Leach et al. describe as 'basically a plot of the constructs from the simple PCA [Principal Components Analysis] … with the elements superimposed' (p. 240).

Fransella et al. (2004) observe that attempts have been made to use a single number which will summarise a grid and allow simple comparisons to be made. A number of such single-figure summaries have been proposed. One line of thought has been to create an index of cognitive complexity. Fransella et al. describe a number of them, including the functionally independent construct (FIC) index devised by Landfield. According to their description, the initial ratings of each element on a scale from − 6 to + 6 were reduced to three levels: negative, zero or positive. The ratings of two elements on two constructs are compared and the number of matches excepting the zero ones are calculated and a correction factor subtracted if the midpoint (zero) ratings were too high. 'Each construct's relationships were then assessed according to a threshold as being functionally independent or not. The degree of functional independence in the grid is the number of functionally independent constructs' (p. 117). Alternative measures include the sum of the rank correlations squared and multiplied by 100 (an intensity measure devised by Bannister), the simple number of constructs, and there are others. Fransella et al. state that 'There is no general agreement that one measure of cognitive complexity/differentiation/integration is better, more useful or more valid than another' (p. 120); the FIC index is understood among personal construct users in North America but not elsewhere. The authors go on to describe a number of other single-figure indices of grids such as measures of extremity (the tendency to use the extreme points on the scales) and element differentiation. It seems many of these have had little use.

All these alternatives are intended to assist the understanding of an individual grid or small sets of grids from one respondent (such as might be obtained before and after therapy).

ANALYSING A SET OF GRIDS

Bell (1997) considers the issue of analysing multiple grids and lists three types of alternative structures which can arise. At one extreme, all grids use the same elements and constructs. At the other, they use the same number of elements but the elements are different and there are different numbers of constructs and the constructs differ. In this latter case, all that can be done is to repeat single grid analysis on each one. But when the grids have the same elements and the same constructs, it is possible to test the communality of construct usage by carrying out a factor analysis and seeing whether the correlations among the elements for that construct are accounted for by a single factor.

Bell (1999) has constructed a program, GRIDSCAL, for analysing multiple repertory grids which have the same elements or same constructs (or both). The program uses individual differences multidimensional scaling (also described as common space analysis). It provides a plot showing the proximity of the elements or constructs and shows the weighting given to each grid included in the analysis.

HOW YOU DO REPERTORY GRID ANALYSIS

As should be clear from what has been said, many forms of analysis can be carried out using a standard statistical package such as SPSS. But there are dedicated grid analysis programs available on the Internet, including Webgrid III (provided by Gaines and Shaw and available at http://gigi.cpsc.ucalgary.ca. (retrieved 24 August 2004)). This provides FOCUS analysis, which sorts a grid for proximity between similar elements and similar constructs. It offers a printout, PRINCOM, which uses principal components analysis to represent a grid in a minimum number of dimensions. Bell provides GRIDSCAL, and there are many other programs available on the Internet. With the rapid changes which are a feature of the Internet, the best advice to offer is that you should simply put 'repgrids' into your favourite search engine and follow the links which it finds.

EXAMPLES OF REPERTORY GRID ANALYSIS AND ITS INTERPRETATION

Here we summarise three studies which have used repertory grids. Fransella et al. (2004) provide a better indication of the range of topics in which repertory grids have been used, as in their Chapter 8 entitled 'Some uses to which grids have been put' they describe studies from a wide range of areas including a clinical setting (itself including anorexia nervosa, depression, suicide, phobias, psychotherapy, nursing), working with children, teaching those with learning difficulties, social relationships, language, use and abuse of drugs, the family, forensic work, market research, careers, sport, organisational applications.

From psychology

Some idea of the complexities which arise when one attempts to use repertory grids in a repeated measures or longitudinal study of a group of respondents is provided by Fournier and Payne (1994) who used them in a study of 56 newly recruited graduates. They administered repertory grids three weeks after the person had started their job and again six months later, using 13 triads of elements so that 13 constructs were elicited from each respondent. The respondents rated each element on each construct using a seven-point scale. In longitudinal studies, it is common to use the constructs obtained at the first presentation on the second one, but Fournier and Payne note that if one is looking at changes in the respondents, expecting to see the development of new constructs in the time interval, then constructs should be elicited on both occasions – though this makes the quantitative analysis of changes difficult.

They devised a classification system, based on the constructs elicited from the graduate employees, which consisted of 35 dimensions. Change in self-image was measured by calculating the difference between 'actual self' on the first occasion (three weeks after the respondent joined the company) and a new element concerning past self ('myself when I joined the company') which was used on the second occasion when the person had been with the employer for six months.

Fournier and Payne report the number of respondents who perceived themselves as having changed or remained stable on each of the 35 dimensions. The authors also tabulate the number of respondents for whom a dimension disappeared between the first and second occasions and the number for whom a new dimension appeared on the second occasion.

Changes in self-esteem were measured by taking the distance between 'actual self' and 'ideal self' on both occasions and the distance between 'past self' and 'ideal self' ratings obtained on the second occasion. Fournier and Payne write: 'Overall, graduates at T2 [i.e. the second testing occasion] have a higher esteem for their actual self than they have for their past self. The paired t test shows that the difference between the average ideal self-past self distance and ideal self-actual self distance at T2 is significant' (p. 309).

From health

Freshwater et al. (2001) used repertory grids in a study of survivors of childhood sexual abuse: 40 women who had been sexually abused in childhood, and 28 who had not, completed a number of measures including rating scales of supplied elements (e.g. self now, ideal self, men in general) and constructs (e.g. trustworthy–untrustworthy). For the clinical group, dyad grids were also completed; here the elements represented the relationships between people (e.g. self to mother). Additional constructs were elicited using the triarchic procedure.

Freshwater et al. examined a number of element relationships including the distance on five supplied constructs between 'self now' and 'ideal self' and the distance between 'men in general' and 'women in general'. The latter is taken to assess sex–role polarisation. The authors report the mean element distances of the 'self' versus 'ideal self' discrepancy and of sex–role polarisation, and note that 'survivors had significantly higher self/ideal self distances than the non-abused group' (p. 387) while there were no significant differences on the sex–role polarisation measure: 'hypothesized differences in sex–role polarization between survivors and others were not found' (p. 390) which 'challenges opinion on the construal patterns of survivors' (p. 391).

From business/management

Langan-Fox and Tan (1997) interviewed 13 managers in a study of organisational culture in Australia; they describe the study as concerned with 'measuring general perceptions of a culture in transition with a public service (government) organization that had recently introduced a new quality service culture' (p. 277). In the interviews, they elicited constructs which were then administered to all the managers. The elicited constructs were subjected to content analysis which identified five main issues which contrasted the established old culture with the desired new one.

These five issues were: industry context, customer orientation, work orientation, motivation, people orientation. From the outcome of the interviews, a questionnaire was constructed asking respondents to rate people who adopted the values of the new culture (described as being 'on the bus'), people who had not fully adopted the new values (described as having 'one foot on the bus') and those reluctant to adopt the new culture (described as 'not on the bus') on 63 items covering the five areas listed above plus 'attitude to the culture change'. Langan-Fox and Tan report the respondents' mean ratings of the three groups and concluded that there was support for the hypothesis: 'that there were significant differences in mean scores of unit managers' perceptions of different culture groups' (p. 285). They took 14 variables which showed significant differences between the three groups and subjected them to cluster analysis; this yielded three clusters: support for trying new ways of doing things, having a constructive solution-oriented approach and having a customer service orientation.

Further details of the study need not concern us, but some of the comments on the value of using repertory grids are worth quoting:

> The initial qualitative approach in this study provided richness in data when uncovering elements of organizational culture from the perspective of its members. This would not have been possible using predetermined culture constructs derived from other studies ... the metaphor ('on the bus') for the culture change would not have been uncovered. (p. 290)
>
> In eliciting constructs, the Rep Grid uncovered culture constructs which were meaningful to members of the culture. The technique was also stimulating and novel. (p. 290)

FAQs

Which elements should be used in a repertory grid?

It should be apparent from what has been said in this chapter that the elements to use will depend on the area of the respondent's construct system which you are investigating. The particular ones may be identified via a preliminary interview programme, as in the Langan-Fox and Tan study described above. Elements should be within the 'range of convenience' of the constructs (i.e. they should be relevant) and should be representative of the area being investigated. This flexibility is one of the benefits of repertory grid methodology, although it also makes it less standardised than many psychological procedures.

How many elements should be used?

There is no precise answer to this question. Kelly used 24 role titles in his original formulation of the Rep test, but Fransella et al. (p. 21) note that 'In most cases, far fewer than 24 elements would be used.' Somewhere between 6 and 12 is not uncommon.

Do you have to use the triarchic procedure for eliciting constructs?

The answer is no; there are alternatives. Fransella et al. (p. 80) point out that 'The grid is truly a technique, and one which is only limited by the user's imagination.' The triarchic procedure is frequently employed, but this chapter is only intended to indicate the flavour of repertory grid technique. If you are seriously intending to use it, you should refer to one of the specialised texts or Internet sources before doing anything else.

How many constructs should I elicit?

Remember that the technique is designated to elicit the respondents' constructs, so the answer lies with them. It is impossible to say in advance how many can be elicited, and will depend in part on the number of elements and triads used. (You may find the respondent has difficulty in expressing additional constructs once they have used the elicitation procedure more than 8 to 10 times.)

SUMMARY

The use of repertory grids is a technique, used in many areas of psychology, for getting respondents to reveal the constructs they use in interpreting the world around them. The usual procedure involves presenting the respondents with sets of three elements and asking which two go together and which is the odd one out, then saying what is the feature which the two that go together have in common: this is the emergent pole of the construct.

Individual repertory grids can be analysed in a number of ways: one can examine the relationships between the constructs or the relationships between elements, and principal components analysis or hierarchical cluster analysis can be used for both. Analysing a set of grids is best done using one of the computer programs devised for the purpose.

GLOSSARY

Construct   a dimension or attribute which a respondent uses in distinguishing between elements. Most constructs are taken to be bipolar.

Contrast pole   the opposite end of a construct from the emergent pole.

Dendrogram a graphical representation of the relationship between elements which illustrates how they form clusters.

Dichotomous grid a grid in which the respondent has indicated whether each element does or does not have the attribute described by the emergent pole of a construct.

Element the entities which are presented to respondents when they are asked to sort them into a group of two and an odd one (in the triarchic method) to reveal their constructs.

Emergent pole the word of phrase which the respondent gives to indicate the feature or attribute which elements have in common.

Repertory grid technique for getting respondents to reveal their constructs by presenting sets of elements and asking how they can be divided.

Triarchic method presenting elements in sets of three and asking the respondent to say which two go together and which is the odd one out.

WHERE TO FIND FURTHER MORE DETAILED INFORMATION

As should be clear, the Internet is the source of a considerable amount of information on personal construct theory and repertory grid procedures. There is no shortage of books on what has proved to be a theory and method of considerable longevity. Bannister and Mair (1968) is an early classic which predates the personal computer. A recent practical guide is provided by Jankowicz (2003) and Fransella et al.'s manual, first published in 1977, has now (2004) been issued in a new edition and includes chapters on computer analysis.

REFERENCES

Bannister, D. and Mair, J.M.M. (1968). *The Evaluation of Personal Constructs*. London: Academic Press.

Bell, R.C. (1997). Using SPSS to analyse repertory grid data. University of Melbourne, Melbourne.

Bell, R.C. (1999). *GRIDSCAL: a Program for Analysing the Data of Multiple Repertory Grids*. Melbourne: R.C. Bell.

Blaikie, N. (2003). *Analyzing Quantitative Data*. London: Sage.

Burr, V. and Butt, T. (1992). *Invitation to Personal Construct Psychology*. London: Whurr.

Fournier, V. and Payne, R. (1994). Change in self-construction during the transition from university to employment: a personal construct psychology approach. *Journal of Occupational and Organizational Psychology*, 67, 279–314.

Fransella, F., Bell, R. and Bannister, D. (2004). *A Manual for Repertory Grid Technique* (2nd edition). Chichester: Wiley.

Freshwater, K., Leach, C. and Aldridge, J. (2001). Personal constructs, childhood sexual abuse and revictimization. *British Journal of Medical Psychology*, 74, 379–397.

Jankowicz, D. (2003). *The Easy Guide to Repertory Grids*. Chichester: Wiley.

Langan-Fox, J. and Tan, P. (1997). Images of a culture in transition: personal constructs of organizational stability and change. *Journal of Occupational and Organizational Psychology*, 70, 273–293.

Leach, C., Freshwater, K., Aldridge, J. and Sunderland, J. (2001). Analysis of repertory grids in clinical practice. *British Journal of Clinical Psychology*, 40, 225–248.

Index